Branding:

The Fast & Easy Way To Create a Successful Brand That Connects, Sells & Stands Out From The Crowd

Thomas Swain

Start Your Week The Right Way

Hey everyone!

Thanks for buying this book. You can keep upto date with me on my YouTube channel. Every week I post new videos about business, lifestyle and success.

Thomas Swain YouTube

It's a way to start your week off with a bang. And fill yourself with ideas that could potentially change everything.

Thomas Swain YouTube

Contents

Introduction 1

Part One: What is a Brand & Why Does it Matter? **6**

What is a Brand? 7

Brand Character 10

Brand Positioning 11

Brand Identity.. 18

Brand Elements.................................... 23

Online Presence.................................... 47

Trademarking Your Brand 51

Brand Guide... 55

Part Two: Market Research & Competitive Analysis.. **61**

Market Research 62

Know Your Audience 66

Survey customers................................... 68

User personas 72

Analyze Competition................................ 76

SWOT competitors 79

Extended Market Research 82

Google... 82

Facebook 85

YouTube... 91

Instagram 93

Amazon 98

Part Three: Unique Branding Strategies Top Brands Use To Thrive 102

Brand Strategy..................................... 103

Pricing Strategies.................................. 113

Pricing Analysis 115

Pricing Strategy 116

Standing Out!....................................... 126

Define Unique Selling Points (USP) 133

USP Best Practices 135

Even more ways to stand out 137

Staying Relevant 147

What Makes Content Go Viral? 150

Viral content example: Psy Gangnam Style

.... 155

Part Four: Driving Brand Loyalty With Emotion… Think Human Experience!..... 159

Brand Journey & Psychology.................. 160

Define a brand journey 162

Brand Psychology 170

Part Five: The Secrets of Building Timeless Brands... 177

Reputation Matters 178

Customer Loyalty 179

Progress Audits 191

Measuring Brand Awareness 197

Common Branding Mistakes................... 200

Conclusion 212

Bonus: Brand Research Examples 221

Brand: Mike Thurston 224

Brand: Tiesto 227

Brand: Bumble 230

Brand: GymShark 233

References 236

Start Your Week The Right Way 239

    Thomas Swain YouTube 239

    Thomas Swain YouTube 240

Introduction

2021, 2022 and onwards...The world we now live in changes and moves at breakneck speed. Everytime we go to buy something we are overwhelmed with advertising, choices from multiple brands. What to buy, where to buy, who to buy from and so on. Those choices we make are influenced by branding and the trust that we have in a brand. Advertising no longer is enough. Nowadays the brand is what sells the product and or services. The brand is what makes it stand out. If a brand has not even been heard of or seen before then obviously sales are going to be difficult. But brands who understand and implement how to do this are able to thrive and stay relevant.

In this book I will show you how to build a successful brand. A brand that will stand out and be trusted with loyal customers. Customers will want to choose your brand over another one. There are specific ways to stand out and we can make use of those ways to trigger positive associations with the brands we build. Humans are deeply affected by stories and you'll learn how to use stories to build emotional connections with your customers. Furthermore I will show you how to define unique selling points and make sure your brand can stand out in any crowded marketplace. It's about having a strong identity combined with a clear understanding of the audience and the market. From then it enables you to create a brand guide with all the essential brand elements. Crafted to perfection right for your target audience.

Now who am I to tell you about brands? First of all I'm someone who studies it every single day. I'm someone who has and puts in the hard work. Not only that. I've actually got proof of success. You can check me out. I've had a successful career as an international tour DJ, producer and best selling author using the brand name Swindali. I've also built a successful brand called History Brought Alive. Both have been proven, clearly defined and profitable.

Before we go any further, let me tell you now there are no shortcuts to this. Building a successful brand is going to require passion and persistence. But in time you'll be able to influence customers to believe in and trust your brand. Selling products and services will then be much easier. Now if you neglect to build a brand it's going to be much more difficult to sell because people just won't know about you. Why would anyone buy something from some random seller? Think about it like this. The purchases you make are usually because you know it works or you know it's good. You know you like it and so you have positive connections to that brand. Now that is a branding at its finest and that's what you will discover in this book. All that plus much more. Such as you will discover how to create a lasting brand with a strategy to make you stand out. You will discover how to set long-term clear goals and guidelines as your brand grows. You will discover how to add value to your customers, engage them and achieve loyalty from them. All of that and much, much more!

Again neglect to brand properly and you will end up with negative associations to your brand. Eventually the brand will just disappear. Take into account the whole of this book. Consider all of it and use it to make smart intentional choices. At the end you will have a compelling story behind your brand and one that is awesome. This will drive purpose, sales and success for the long-term future. Whether you have just started out or you have an existing brand that needs to shake things up you're going to find value here. So without further ado I welcome you to branding.

Part One: What is a Brand & Why Does it Matter?

What is a Brand?

A brand is more than a logo and a name. It's also more than the way it looks or what is sold. Those are just some of the many elements of a brand. A brand is omnipresent in everything it does. From its interactions with customers to it's marketing materials, imagery, online presence and much more. A brand stands for making a promise on what people believe it is. Furthermore a brand accounts for attributes of a product or service which cannot be seen. They are more abstract such as the emotions resulting from using a brand. Whilst you might not be fully aware of this it is true that we associate emotionally with brands. For example you might associate fashion brands with status. Or you might associate a particular skin brand with youthfulness. Such emotional associations are not explicitly told by brand. Rather they are subliminally communicated through the themes and content of the brand. This is powerful because it influences how people perceive a brand. Brands may want to be perceived in certain ways. Maybe they want to be perceived as innovative. Or maybe they want to be perceived as cool and trendy. In the simplest terms according to British advertising tycoon, David Mackenzie Ogilvy CBE, a brand is "The Intangible Sum of a Product's Attributes"

Building a successful brand requires passion and persistence. Then they become established by building trust and belief in their promises. Effective branding works on influencing consumers to believe in a brand. Strong brands create trust and emotional connections with their target audiences. Naturally this makes selling much easier because people tend to buy from brands which they trust and believe in.

Without a brand it will be more difficult to sell. Branding is what people will first be impressed with when they are introduced to a business. Would you buy some no name computer? Or would you buy the one with a good reputation? Probably the latter and you're probably willing to spend more on it. People don't want to buy something from some random seller with no personality or information. Now more than ever building trust and recognition is essential. With all the new businesses competing everyday it is the ones with strong branding that stand out and thrive for years. Consumers will be more likely to stay loyal to a brand if it meets their needs. They will keep buying their new products or services and add ons. Plus it will keep them profitable long into the future.

Brand Character

Brand character is a set of human characteristics and attributes that give a brand its unique standing in the market and in consumers minds. Essentially it is the personality of a brand. It helps the consumer to relate to a brand on an emotional level. In turn this helps brands to position their unique selling points, values and fundamentals. Some brands for example are perceived as being serious and sophisticated. Then some are perceived as being more youthful and fun. Such things can make brands iconic in the public eye. When taking steps toward defining a brand character consider some of the following questions.

- What adjectives would people use to describe it?
- If asked to describe it in one sentence what would people say?
- What kinds of words do customers use when posting reviews?

- If you could choose five descriptive words what would they be?

Answering these questions is important because it will help you to define a brand character that is consistent and connects emotionally. Otherwise it won't be clear enough and the message can easily get diluted. Again standing out is paramount. Having a strong identity makes that possible.

Brand Positioning

Brand positioning ultimately will be the difference between being an iconic brand or just another brand in a crowded market. Brand positioning according to renowned marketing author, consultant, and professor Phillip Kotler is "the act of designing the company's offering and image to occupy a distinctive place in the mind of the target market".

Essentially how a brand positions itself is how it stands out from its competitors. This should be easy to explain in a few sentences. Why is your brand better? Now that could be its unique selling proposition (USP). For example that could be "it tastes better" or "it's a perfect fit". Take time to figure out the USP because it is an important part of the branding process that will help sales and connections with customers.

Through shaping consumer preferences via brand association it influences their purchasing decisions. A successful brand positioning strategy will be perceived in a positive and credible way in the minds of consumers. In order to succeed with brand positioning some of the following information needs to be gathered and considered.

- Understanding what customers want
- Understanding the capabilities of the brand

- Understanding positioning of competing brands

With more information gathered and considered you can move onto creating a brand positioning statement. This should resonate with your customers, be able to be honoured by your brand and stand out from the competition. Consider defining your brand position in three words. But avoid using generic words. Be specific in your summary.

Finally with those points covered your challenge is to then reflect this brand position in all that the brand does and represents. From its visual identity to its marketing, communications and so on. Below are some examples of how some famous brands have positioned themselves.

Tesla

Tesla positions itself as a luxury car brand with a focus on the quality of their vehicles. Additionally they position themselves as being long range, electronic and eco friendly. Standing out from the competition is easily achieved since they are different from standard vehicles due to the fact that they are electronic. Furthermore they promote uniqueness through adverts and unique features such as "Ludicrous Mode." Here's how they match up to the four points.

- Understanding what customers want - Luxury
- Understanding the capabilities of the brand - Eco friendly
- Understanding positioning of competing brands - Unique
- Brand position in three words - Luxury, eco friendly & unique

Nike is a sports clothing brand with a focus on innovation and performance. They target serious athletes and markets looking to enhance their performance. In fact the name Nike comes from the Greek Goddess of Victory and their tagline "Just Do It" encapsulates that. Advertising campaigns focus on athletes getting the job done and succeeding. This promotes their position of being the best you can be. Here's how they match up to the four points.

- Understanding what customers want - Performance
- Understanding the capabilities of the brand - Achievement
- Understanding positioning of competing brands - Innovation
- Brand position in three words - Performance, achievement & innovation

Apple

Apple is a technology brand that stands out in a strong way. They build innovative and stylish technology which strongly resonates with their consumers' needs. They have successfully created rapport with their customers who associate with being innovative, creative and imaginative, just like Apple. Instead of focusing on price they focus on values and connection with their customers. Here's how they match up to the four points.

- Understanding what customers want - Understanding
- Understanding the capabilities of the brand - Value
- Understanding positioning of competing brands - Connection
- Brand position in three words - Understanding, value & connection

As you can see, brand positioning will help to identify customers and influence the brand into their mind. Naturally this will maximize the brand's relevance to them. Focus on adding value and making it appealing to them. Brands must be unique and offer competitive value in the marketplace. Do your research. Learn about the market you're in and what your competition is doing. Think about how you can stand out. Later we will look at this more in more detail.

Brand Identity

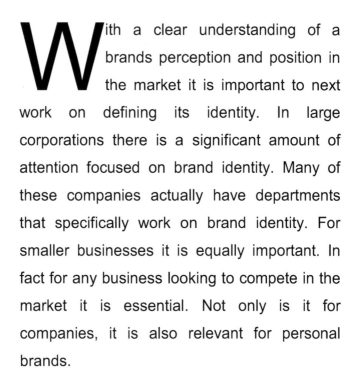

With a clear understanding of a brands perception and position in the market it is important to next work on defining its identity. In large corporations there is a significant amount of attention focused on brand identity. Many of these companies actually have departments that specifically work on brand identity. For smaller businesses it is equally important. In fact for any business looking to compete in the market it is essential. Not only is it for companies, it is also relevant for personal brands.

Brand identity is defined by its vision or in other words why it exists, what it does and the values it holds. For a new brand it's a good idea to work on defining these before anything else. Incidentally this in time may evolve. When a brand is first launched it is an unknown entity. For any established business it is essential to understand how its brand is presented publicly. To begin with, evaluate the core of the brand's identity. Why does the brand exist? What are its values and mission? What's most important to the brand? It's a good idea to display these on the company website and even in its office to ensure it's clear to all those working with the brand.

Brand identity consists of a number of visual elements which include the following.

- A logo or wordmark
- Typefaces and treatments
- Consistent content and images
- Unique colors and palette
- Library of graphics
- Visual online identity

Additional branding terms to be aware of include.

- Brand assets – the visual elements such as colors, fonts and so on.
- Brand associations – the things that are associated with a brand.
- Brand awareness – how easy it is for customers to identify a brand in the market.
- Brand personality – personality traits of a brand such as cool, trendy or innovative.
- Brand positioning – how a brand positions itself in a market.
- Brand promise – the unique selling point of a brand.
- Brand values – what a brand lives upto.
- Brand voice – the way in which a brand communicates.

When designing a brand identity it would be an excellent idea to work with a graphic designer. Having such a professional on board will help to turn your creative ideas into reality. The creative elements will represent the look, feel and voice of the brand's identity. These will then be communicated in the marketing, production and services of the brand. Brand elements create the identity of a brand. Designing those requires researching and understanding the market and how the brand fits into it. Here are six points to consider.

- Make it memorable – the elements of a brand's identity should attract the attention of customers. This works well through simplicity and in turn being easy to remember or recognize.
- Make it meaningful – brand elements should have a meaning that communicates the brand's identity. In

turn this should inform the customer and build a relationship with them.

- Make it likable – brand elements should leave a positive impression. Make sure they are likeable and pleasing.
- Make it transferable – consider if the brand elements work across different mediums such as social media, business cards and so on. Does it translate well in different regions?
- Make it adaptable – great brand elements should be able to stand the test of time. Being able to adapt with changes in trends and tastes make it possible.
- Make it protectable – whatever you choose you should legally protect it. Not only from being copied but to make sure you have the rights to use it. Be sure to pay due diligence to this.

Now let's take a closer look at brand elements.

Brand Elements

Brand name

A brand name is the word or phrase that identifies a product, company, service or concept of a business. On the surface most big brand names look simple. However, coming up with an iconic and memorable name can be difficult. Consider brand names such as Snickers, Porsche, Armani, Netflix and so on. Amazingly they have pretty much become part of everyday language. As such consumers are prepared to pay more for such names.

A good brand name sets the groundwork for having a solid brand identity. After all, the name is the first impression customers and prospects have of it. If it brings up a negative or non reaction then it's not good. The name should convey what you want the brand to represent and stand out from the competition. Be sure it is authentic and represents the brand. Once you have chosen a name stick with it. Here are some more points to consider when choosing a name.

1. Authentic

Well chosen brand names reflect what a product or service is about. Such names can help consumers remember the brand. Consumers desire brands that are authentic and represent what they are about. That's why it's important that the name fits with the concept and essence of the brand. Consider the following questions.

- What are the brand values?
- Why does the brand do what it does?
- What is different about the brand?

Ultimately the brand name should be relevant to its products or services. Don't just base it on keywords or generic terminology. If you get stuck try using some of the business name generators found on a Google search.

Great brand names are easy to say and remember. Brand names won't mean much if people forget them. Follow the principles of making it simple to keep it memorable. Having simplicity as a feature of the name makes this possible. Make it easy to pronounce and understand. That should be universal regardless of language. Shorter names tend to work better in this regard. Also a short and simple brand name can be printed off with less space, and is easier to recognize. In addition, alliteration is a great way to make names more memorable. Alliteration means the occurrence of the same letter or sound at the start of connected words. For example Coca-Cola or Top-Shop.

3. Timeless

Choosing a brand name requires time and effort. Make sure you spend that time wisely on choosing a name that will last as the business evolves. Don't make the mistake of choosing something seasonal or based on a hot trend. The name should be evergreen and flexible enough to deal with business developments.

4. Avoid obscenity

Obscene language or symbols should be avoided at all costs. This will only spoil a brand's reputation. It might seem cool but ultimately it will be likely to put people off.

Tag line

"Breakfast of Champions" by Wheaties and "The Best a Man Can Get" by Gillette are catchy taglines that perfectly capture the brand's identity and purpose. They quickly state the brand's concept and offer value to the customer. This makes them want to be associated with it. Plus they are timeless. Tag lines should be easy to say, memorable and convey your brand personality. Don't overthink this. Again it should be simple. Once you decide on a tag line, stick with it. Just as your company will stick to its promises.

Logo

In simple terms a logo is the visual trademark that identifies a brand. It is usually a small piece of artwork created to represent a brand. That could be an image or a wordmark which is a combination of fonts and colors. For example the Google logo. Some logos have become so iconic that they don't need words to be recognized. Just think of the McDonalds "M" or the Adidas emblem. You know the brand without the words. Now that is brand association at its finest!

Keep it simple. Less is more. Most iconic brands utilize this concept. Choosing or designing a logo is a creative process. Make sure that it represents what you want the public to recognize your brand for. Careful consideration and group think should be applied here. So what makes a well designed logo?

- It represents the brand
- It is easily recognizable
- It is versatile
- It is timeless

These four points are important. In summary the logo should represent the brand, be easy to recognize, and be versatile enough so that it can be used in the marketing and designs whilst also being timeless. That means it is not confined to current trends. Every design choice or consideration of a logo should tick those four boxes. The winner will be a clear representation of the four points. Here are some more things to consider.

Size - Larger objects draw more attention and make them seem more important.

Perception - In the west of the world people read from left to right. As such whatever appears on the left side of the logo will be perceived as the most important. Consider your region of business.

Space - When items are loosely spaced it creates a negative perception. Be careful not to leave too much space.

Placement - Having a random placement creates a playful perception, whilst more symmetry creates formal perception.

Symbols - One of the earliest forms of communication was achieved through symbols. Thousands of years ago cave walls were covered in hieroglyphics and those have evolved into the printed word. Symbols can be used to convey information and represent messages or concepts. Just think of X marks the spot or the skull and crossbones near an electricity hazard. For brands they can be a powerful way of communicating what's important to the identity. Think about The Nike swoosh, it is recognized worldwide and is associated with the brand. Symbols can indeed become iconic. Such iconic symbols strongly represent brand identity and reinforce it in the consumers minds.

When choosing symbols just be sure to research the cultural and general interpretations of any you choose. Symbols are not only eye-catching there is also psychology behind them. When designing symbols, have an intent behind what you wish to convey. Is it friendly? Maybe it's strong? Or maybe its intelligence? For example logos convey security and stability. Alternatively use figures or come up with something new. Work with a design team to ensure your goals are met.

Forms and shapes

Shapes are powerful. All logos have a shape. Shapes communicate messages. There are three major categories of shapes. Each has their own psychological associations.

Geometric shapes - Geometric shapes are those unnatural and precise shapes such as squares, circles, and triangles. Since these are not natural they are good at communicating power and order.

- Squares and rectangles: communicate strength and reliability.
- Circles: communicate unity and harmony.

31

- Curves: communicate gentleness and softness.
- Triangles communicate different meanings based on whether they face up or down. When right side up: communicate power and stability.
- When pointed down: communicate downward momentum.
- When pointing to the side: communicate movement and direction in the way they are facing.

Abstract or symbolic shapes - Abstract or symbolic shapes represent something to a culture. They have clear meaning and are great at conveying a message without words. Since the images are seen often then logos should be smart about how they use them. Here are some examples.

- Stars: communicate religion and patriotism.

- Hearts: communicate love.
- Broken hearts: communicate sadness.
- Arrows: communicate movement, and direction.

Organic shapes - Organic shapes are those shapes that represent items in nature. For example leaves, trees, water and so on. This category also includes irregular shapes that are not natural. Such shapes are not defined by exact dimensions or regular patterns. They are more random and natural. Incidentally there are a number of associations with each organic shape. So choose wisely. For example choosing trees or water will have its own communication of emotion. Make sure that matches the brand concept.

Lines - Lines can be used to create definition, form and direction. Aesthetically they can have a psychological impact.

- Thin lines: communicate elegance and the feminine.
- Thick lines communicate strength and the masculine.
- Straight lines: communicate order and structure.
- Curved lines: communicate energy.
- Jagged/zig-zagging lines: communicate tension.
- Irregular lines: communicate playfulness.

The Significance of Color

Color goes much deeper than what the eye can see. According to scientific data people subconsciously judge a product within ninety seconds. Based on that judgment upto ninety percent is influenced by color. The emotions that color can evoke is a necessity that great branding needs to pay attention to. The effect of color on human psychology should not be underestimated. Consider some of the following suggestions and think about the kind of brands they would match well with.

Bright colours   - Attracts attention and is excellent at encouraging people to purchase quickly. Less bright colors can influence loyalty and trust.

Blue - Associated with trust, calm and stability.

Red - Associated with power and love in positive ways. Or in a negative context with risk or danger. Very attention demanding.

Green - Associated with calmness, nature and good fortune.

Black and White - A confident association that can work on creating striking contrasts between colors. White on the other hand can be more peaceful.

Yellow - Associated with positive and energetic moods.

Purple - Associated with mystery and spirituality.

Pink - Associated with feminine and is an affectionate color.

Furthermore mixing colors also has psychological influence. For example,

Mixing bright colors - Associated with energy and youthfulness.

Black and white mix - Associated with maturity and sophistication.

Monochromatic - Associated with a unified feel.

Consider some of the above suggestions and do your own work on researching more about color psychology when designing a brand. Choose colors that represent your brand and the emotions that you want to elicit. They should represent the brand personality. Customers want authenticity. Look at how the arches of McDonalds are associated with strength and authority. The main colors used are bright, eye-catching yellow and red. Red colors trigger stimulation and hunger. This also attracts attention. Whilst yellow is a color that is easy to see in daylight and helps to be seen from distance. Strong brand identity at its finest.

Finally, be aware of how color is interpreted in different regions and cultures. If necessary make adjustments. Sometimes for other regions it would be wise to make alternative

37

designs. Be sure the brand is getting exactly the right associations and intent you desire it to be perceived with.

Typography

Typography has an important influence over how people perceive a brand and its messaging. Fonts can convey more than just the words that are written. In fact, personality can be represented through it. Furthermore, studies by MIT psychologist Kevin Larson have discovered that designs with good typography take less time to read and create a "stronger sense of clarity."

Fonts impact people and therefore brands need to focus on choosing the right type of personality to convey. Take for example the Serif and Sans Serif fonts. These were originally designed to make reading easier. Naturally these make a good choice for many brands.

Choosing fonts that are easier to read will be more user friendly and as such result in happier customers. For brands looking for something bolder or quirkier they may consider other fonts. But those would be for more niche businesses.

Whatever font the brand decides upon ultimately it should align with customer expectation of the brand. Take a look at some fonts. Try matching their feelings to the feelings and perception of the brand. Choose fonts that represent it well. Or perhaps you're not sure and can't find a font. Try working with a graphic designer. If the font is a unique one created specifically for the brand then license it.

Fonts come in four major categories:

Serif
- Feature: short lines coming off the letter edges.
- Perception: traditional, stable and formal.

- Examples: Garamond, Georgia, Times New Roman

Serifs are a great choice if a large amount of text is going to be used. This makes it easier to read. For brands that want to convey authority and prestige they are an excellent choice.

Sans-serif
- Feature: letters with serifs.
- Perception: fun and casual.
- Examples: Calibri, Helvetica, Roboto.

Sans-serif fonts also make for an easy reading experience. For online content they work particularly well. For brands that make use of blogs and websites or have casula business cultures they are a great fit.

Handwritten
- Feature: letters that mimic handwriting.
- Perception: personal connection

- Examples: Apple's Noteworthy, Insolente, Pacifico.

Handwritten fonts are a good choice if a brand wants to make a more personal connection with their customers. They are a great choice for conveying elegance and a personalized touch.

Decorative
- Feature: unique letters
- Perception: stylish, creative and quirky.
- Examples: Bangers, Limelight, Unkempt.

Decorative fonts are usually custom creations. They are a great choice for brands that want to stand out as being unique and to ramp up their personality. For logo designs they work particularly well and can be easily tuned to match the personality of the brand.

Design

The design of a brand brings it to our attention instantly. Heinz ketchup uses a classic design style giving it a homely feel. They use bright red colors to satiate the taste buds and association with tomato flavor. Red bull utilizes a clean sleek design with powerful colors that associate with its sharp energizing drink. Whilst design is not a logo it serves to further identify a brand and associate it positively with consumers. Carefully select colors, typography, fonts and design to match with your brand identity.

Illustration

For some businesses illustration works well as forming a part of their brand identity. Illustrations could be things such as graphics to communicate style and grace. Or for example they could be cool elements to add to a polish off a brand. Overall they are building a stronger, more unique identity. When choosing illustrations make sure they compliment the identity of the brand. Don't go too overboard. Keep it simple and memorable.

Email design

Making a good first impression is important. Nowadays for brands that first impression can often come from email. A welcome email to a prospect is the first exchange between them and your brand. Make sure the email setsa the tone for a good relationship. Take the time to design the email. Make use of a signature and all the important information with it. In addition, be consistent with the communication style so that it represents the brand voice.

Business cards

Some may think business cards to be outdated but they are still important. For those times when you may be out networking then a business card can leave a lasting reminder with the person you talked with. They will serve as a physical reminder of you and your brand to them. Make sure that your brand elements are consistent on the design. Usually that would be colors, typography and logo.

Product packaging

If the brand makes physical products then the designs and packaging of those products need to reflect the brand identity. Not only that but it needs to stand out when it is placed with all the competition in a market. Let it speak for you when you're not there.

The physical shape of a brand if it is a product is something that becomes unique to it. Consider how Apple makes visually aesthetic products or the shape of a Heineken beer bottle. There is considerable thought going into these which further identify the brand. Shape is an easy way to stand out from the competition. Just imagine a rack of beer bottles. Most look the same. If you tweak the shape a little then it will be more eye catching and attention grabbing. Innovative creative thinking is the way forward.

Senses

Sound, smell, touch and taste are also all key elements of a brand. Depending on the relevance it makes sense to make these unique to each brand. Apple has their own unique sounds to their products. Whilst some adverts for products feature catchphrases. "Because you're worth it". Then there's how some brands have their own unique smells. Aftershave being the perfect example. You smell it, you want it. Coffee shops utilize this well. Moving on taste is a crucial element of branding in the food industry. Food and beverage companies are well known for perfecting the crunchiness, chewiness and flavours of their products to deeply connect with consumers.

Voice

A brand isn't only about visual elements. The way a brand communicates or rather its voice also needs to be designed. What is a brand voice? How a brand talks to its customers and its style of communication are its brand voice. Just like we communicate with friends and family in certain ways brands have their own ways with their audiences. This depends on the target audience of a brand. It should represent them and also the brand values. Consumers invest into their relationship with a brand that connects emotionally. So how can brands develop a voice?

To begin with it is necessary to establish the core of a brand identity. This encompasses its vision, values, mission and what makes it stand out from the competition. To get you started choose three descriptions. Those are words that evoke emotions. Consider what kind of mood and emotion you wish your brand to elicit.

46

Understand your audience. Get to know about who they are. Establish a tone that speaks to them. That will require some trial and error to get onto the right path. Just be prepared to make adjustments.

Online Presence

One of the most effective ways of engagement with customers is through having an online presence. Now more than ever customers search for and then buy what they want online. According to research by Salesforce, almost eight five percent of consumers research online before they make a purchase. Needless to say, brands should implement a strong online strategy to achieve success.

An online presence is the place for brands to engage with their consumers. This allows brands to create their own narrative and stand out in the market. Included in an online presence is not just a website. It is also social media, reviews and the conversations with consumers. Through all of this consumers can discover what a brand is about and engage with it on a more personal level. This can serve to make a brand more credible in addition to increasing awareness of it.

Website

The first step to take when building a strong online presence is to create a professional looking and user friendly website. A professional looking website with a relevant domain is essential to the online element of a successful brand. Use your website presence like a display window in a shop. The website for a brand serves as being a home for customers and prospects to learn more about it. Customers can then decide on whether the brand is credible and trustworthy through the website.

Identify industry standards for websites. Focus on having a strong and well designed website that conveys the reputation you strive for. Make sure design elements are used consistently. If you're on a busy street you want to attract customers with the most attractive designs and displays. Show them who you are and what you do quickly and attractively. Keep them simple, great looking and easy to use. Make use of SEO and analytics to stand out. Professional services should be hired for this. Additionally the website should offer value and outstanding content. Make sure it is all up to date and relevant to the market. News and updates can be shared here and a blog page is great for this.

Social media

Combine that with upto date and engaging social media and you're onto a full presence. A strong online presence should include active social media channels. In recent times social media has exploded. Nowadays you cannot have a brand without it. People are spending more and more time online and especially on social media. Quite simply it has become a necessity for brands. This will help your brand to stay more relevant and deliver to audiences.

Research what similar brands use in the market. Some social media platforms may be more relevant than others for particular niches. Make the most of them. The major ones right now of course are Instgaram, Twitter, Facebook and TikTok. Depending on your business depends on the platform. However, try experimenting with them and go with what gets the most traction.

Social media channels should be active and consistent. Customers will check out a brand's online presence in order to get an idea of their reputation. You need to be active and engaging on these platforms so as to maximize customers. Work on increasing engagement and followers. Consistently post content and engaging posts to bring more and more traffic. Stay up to date and stay relevant.

Trademarking Your Brand

With a name and elements chosen you need to make sure that you can legally use them. It should be possible to obtain the full legal rights in whatever countries and regions your business operates in. Confirm if any other companies use that name. Consult with The United States Patent and Trademark Office and the WIPO Global Brand online databases to discover if using a name is possible. Additionally you can consult with attorneys that specialize in trademark law. Be thorough in the process so that you don't get stung later. In addition search on domain name service providers to see if there are any websites with the brand name in it. Also search on social media for pages using the name.

In order to protect the name you choose it is important that you register and trademark the name. A trademark according to the United States Patent and Trademark Office (USPTO), is "a word, phrase, symbol, and/or design that identifies and distinguishes the source of the goods of one party from those of the others." The process of registering a trademark is easy to do and can be achieved in three simple steps.

1. Search

To begin with, search the federal database to find out if the name you wish to trademark is already in use or not. Use the USPTO's

Trademark Electronic Search System to search for the name or similar names.

https://www.uspto.gov/trademarks/search

2. Apply

Once a search has been completed and nothing has been found similar or the same then you can move forward with a trademark application. This will allow you to file for the permission to use the name commercially and to prevent others doing the same. There will be a small fee required.

3. File

Once the application has been completed you can file for either TEAS Plus or TEAS Standard. The Plus option has a lower rate of rejection and is less expensive. However it will require a custom description of any services or goods. otherwise the Standard option may be more suitable. After submitting the application The USPTO will send a receipt and a serial number that can be used to check the application status.

Brand Guide

A brand guide is a blueprint for the team members of a brand to follow anytime they create or design content for that brand. It ensures that the brand identity is correctly represented in a consistent way. An identity of a brand often changes and evolves through time. However the personality for the most part stays the same. This is where having a guideline helps to authentically stay true to that personality. When creating a brand guide, consider answers to the following questions.

- What assets does the brand have available for publicity?
- How should the brand be perceived?
- What typography and fonts does the brand use?
- What colors does it use?

- What logos does it use for each platform?
- What style of voice does the brand use?
- What images does the brand use?

Having answers to these key questions will help the brand to grow. As new employees join the team they can refer to the guide. It's likely that the brand will be creating lots of content and that will all need to be guided. In addition if the brand hires external contractors they can also benefit from using the guide. Members of the team from the top to the bottom should follow the brand guide.

There are six essential items that form a complete brand guide.

1. Brand Overview
- About the brand
- Goals and vision of the brand

2. Brand Logo

- An aesthetic representation of the brand identity

3. Brand Color Palette

- The colors the brand uses. What is permitted and what is not.

4. Brand Typography

- The typeface and font of the brand. Plus how to use headers, headings and so on.

5. Brand Images

- Image guidelines for the brand. Within a brand guide there should be specifications on images. Those should include what kind of images to be used and what not to use. Include sources, sizes, qualities and so on. Images should also be specified to have a certain aesthetic. That could be certain filters or defintiations. Maybe it's the content of the images also. Whatever it is that matters, put it in the brand guideline.

6. Brand Voice

- How the brand interacts with customers and the public. Its style of voice. Ultimately these will serve as guidelines to create consistently for the brand.

Stay consistent

When a brand is inconsistent it dilutes the identity of the brand. People lose track of it and it becomes forgotten into obscurity. Make sure the brand is first clearly defined and then be consistent with it in the guide and so on. Target audiences are responsive to familiarity and predictability. Lock in those brand qualities and make sure all team members stick with the plan. Focus on being consistent. Consider some of the following points to achieve brand consistency.

- Does the brand have a consistent visual design?

Colors, styles and fonts should be the same across all platforms, websites and materials. Visually consistent brands are memorable.

- Does the brand have a consistent style of messaging?

A strong brand identity relies on consistent communication. That comes directly from the values and strategy of the brand. The message should not be diluted. It should be clear and people should know what it's about.

- Does the brand deliver in a consistent way?

The promises a brand makes must consistently meet the realities of customers. Failure to deliver on promises creates a bad reputation. As such the brand will suffer.

- Does the brand consistently resonate with its audience?

No matter how good the brand identity looks and is, if it doesn't consistently resonate with the target market then it's destined to fail. Keep an eye on keywords and how they perform. Keep an eye on customer engagement and satisfaction.

Part Two: Market Research & Competitive Analysis

Market Research

Now before anything is designed or formally decided upon it's important to conduct thorough research. How a brand fits in the market, its customers, competitors and metrics all need to be analyzed. For new brands and for existing brands looking to develop this is equally as important. Before you start selling anything online or even talking with manufacturers I highly recommend you research whether or not there is enough demand for your business. It doesn't matter how great you or your friends and family think an idea is. The reality is that you need solid facts and enough evidence that proves your business is going to be worth investing time and money into. However don't worry because such research doesn't take that long. Plus it is fairly easy and in most cases can be free to do.

First off a SWOT analysis can help to understand the brand and how it operates. Through examining the brand's strengths, weaknesses, opportunities, and threats, new ideas and strategies can be discovered. Use a grid system just like on the following page to fill in each quadrant with the information relevant to it.

Strengths:	**Weaknesses:**
- The positive factors of the brand - What is unique about the brand? - Are there any ways or areas in which it excels?	- The negative factors of the brand - Are there any areas where it performs poorly? - What are the weaknesses? - Is it well

63

- Is it well funded? - How does it benefit the customer? - Is it a good idea?	funded? - Are the employees good? - Is the customer happy?
Opportunities: - What opportunities exist? - Can you fill a gap in the market? - Can you partner with someone? - Can you outperform a competitor? - Do you benefit from any trends or regulations? - Do you benefit from any technological or other advantages? - Can you improve on	**Threats:** - What threats exist? - What do your rivals offer that you can't? - Are your rivals more popular? - Are there any regulations or economic issues? - Are there any disadvantages? - What could go wrong? - What would you do to resolve it?

something?	

Know Your Audience

Customers will either make or break a brand. Customers should be at the heart of any successful brand. All successful brands have an excellent understanding of their audience. Each brand will have its own unique customers with differing desires and needs. Brands that resonate with their customers have successfully uncovered their drives. Therefore you need to understand who they are. Discover this and you will be able to meet and fulfill their desires.

First of all, find the audience who might be interested in your products or services. Their reasons for buying will vary. Building a strong brand identity comes from understanding the wants and needs of the target audience. Work on discovering who they are. Be specific and accurate in your audience analysis. You never want to be selling to people who are not interested. That will only result in customer dissatisfaction and end with a bad reputation. At the very least you will need to consider the following.

- Demographics
- Gender
- Age
- Education
- Occupation
- Interests and hobbies
- What do they do?
- Why do they buy?
- What's their budget?
- What are their expectations?

Obtaining this information can be achieved via a number of ways. First of all you can go about interviewing people who you think fit your ideal customer profile. Talk to previous customers, competitors and employees. Alternatively you can try focus groups or use tools such as Google Analytics or some of the metrics provided on social media. Get the research phase done right and people will stay engaged with your brand.

Once you have a clear picture of your target audience you need to share that across your whole business. All people working in the business need to be aware of the target audience. Employees are brand ambassadors and they need to be able to effectively communicate with the target audience.

Survey customers

To help build a clearer strategy, survey your potential customers. There are a number of ways to collect information. When you survey people it's important to at first go broad. Begin with surveying any existing customers. Don't shy away from negative experiences. Survey those customers who had both positive and negative experiences with your business. It will all help to build a full picture. Moving on, survey potential prospects. Those are the people who have yet to have any experience with your business. New insights and a fresh look on things should come from them. Next, make use of referrals. Ask any of your contacts to connect you with potential candidates to survey.

Customer feedback surveys

Customer feedback surveys are proven ways to gather information from customers. Make use of companies such as SurveyMonkey or TypeForm who specialize in surveys. Keep your surveys short and simple so that they get a higher retention. In addition make sure to brand the surveys using elements of the brand identity.

Email and feedback forms

Creating a form on your brand website or instore gives customers a chance to leave feedback. The same can be achieved via leaving a link in emails. Focus on simplicity and ease of use, again for higher retentions.

Direct contact

Forms and surveys are a simple solution but many people are not so motivated to complete them. However, reaching out to customers directly is a great way to get instant feedback. Follow up on sales and prospects. Get their feedback on your products and services.

Usability tests

When launching a new product or service there are going to be some problems and troubleshooting along the way. The best solution is to get feedback from the target market of the products or services. Reach out to potential customers to test your ideas. Get their feedback and use it to improve.

Social media

Social media is where most people tend to congregate online. The platforms are fully engaged so make use of them. Pose questions, surveys and opinion polls to gather useful feedback. There are various integrated polling and feedback tools on social media. Make the most of them.

Customer service

If your business is a larger one then it is a good idea to have a specific team dedicated to customer relations and services. When customers have complaints or queries the team will be there for them. Take note of feedback from the team and have direct communication with them. This will give you insights and help to continually improve your brand.

Website data

Websites offer analytics data that will offer numerous customer insights. This includes everything from where they came from, keywords they used, time spent browsing and much more. Essentially the analytics data will provide enough information about how the customer came to you and why. Useful indeed.

User personas

After surveying customers, gathering data and research, move on to creating a user persona. In marketing terminology this is a made up identity to provide a detailed description of a target customer. It should be thoroughly researched and include detailed information such as demographics, hobbies, gender, interests and so on.

Creating a persona will help you to:

- Identify who your customers are
- What their pain points and goals are
- How they spend their time
- When they are most active
- Their behaviours
- Their buying choices

Imagine your perfect customer. It helps to get really detailed here. Consider their age, sex, financial status, demographics. Use your earlier research. Depending on what industry your brand is in you will want to consider additional information. For example if you're in the music business then certainly customer music genre preference is important. Or if for example you're in the beverage industry then the health and lifestyle factors of customers would be important. With a persona created, businesses will have the knowledge on how to create the most effective branding strategy for potential customers. The essentials of a persona are as follows.

- Age – Determining customer age will affect many choices.
- Job – Are they employed? Are they studying? These are important points.
- Demographic – Where do they live?
- Goals – What are their needs and wants? How do they relate to your business?
- Pain points – In relation to your products and services what are their main problems?
- Keywords - Choose words that summarize the personality traits of the person. Use tools such as Google Keyword planner to find more.
- Channels – Where does this person frequent online? How do they get information? Where do they buy?

Imagine your personas as characters in a story. Do they identify with your brand? Personas can help ultimately to build a coherent identity. This will keep your brand focused on the correct goals.

Analyze Competition

Building a strong brand identity also requires a detailed understanding of the competition. All markets are competitive. Brands should be aware of this fact and analyze the competition. First of all identify who your competitors are. There will be direct and indirect competitors. Direct would be those who do exactly what you do. Whilst indirect would be those who offer something similar but target a different need. For example weight loss for women vs weight loss for pensioners.

Find out where your competitors are. This can be discovered through careful and thorough research. Start researching what other brands in your niche are selling. Who are your competitors? Find out how well they are doing.

What is the market size? Has it changed much recently? Take a look at their brand identities. Define metrics to compare. Gather the data and analyze it. Make use of Google, Linkedin and social media. Look at what they are currently doing. Are they making changes in strategy or price? Take note of their strategies. Additionally analyze their rankings, content, branding and engagement of competitors. Take a look at their marketing campaigns and advertising efforts. Analyze their online presence. Assess their marketing and advertising materials and efforts. Some of the metrics you should consider are the following. Be sure to record your data in a spreadsheet.

Who are your competitors? - First of all, research who else is competing in your market.

Analyze your competitors' social media. - Do they have a strong following? How many followers do they have? Are they getting good engagement? What are they doing well? What are they not doing well?

Are there many reviews of your competitors' products online? - If you find many reviews that's a good sign because clearly people are buying their products. Therefore there is demand. Additionally you can even look at the reviews to see what the customers like and don't like. All of this will help you to create great offers for your customers.

How long have your competitors been active? - Use WHOis.net and enter their URL. This will give you their website creation date. If they have been around for a while then this is another sign that the niche is strong and healthy.

Are there mostly big companies or smaller ones? Can you compete? - If your niche is dominated by big players then it will be hard to compete. But if you notice lots of thriving smaller players then it's a good sign you can compete. Overall you want to be looking for low competition and high demand. Low competition would mean lots of smaller players or less players. Whilst high demand would mean good results of traffic and many reviews. Use the following research tools to help you make good decisions.

- SpyFu: Find out the keywords that a competitor is using.
- Google Trends: Find out what the latest trends are in your target market.
- Google Alerts: Make use of alerts to find out what customers are saying about the competition.

SWOT competitors

Select the three to five competitors from your research and run through a SWOT of them.

- Strengths. What are their Strengths? What keeps people coming back? - For example; high number of subscribers, strong branding, etc

- Weaknesses. What are their Weaknesses? What puts people off? - For example; poor engagement, low quality videos, etc

- Opportunities. What are their Opportunities? How could they improve? - For example; easy to link with products, could offer in other languages, etc

- Threats. What are their Threats? What could put them out of business? - For example; could get censored, competitive market, etc

To help you with SWOT analysis put your results into a 4X4 grid with a box for each of the acronyms.

Extended Market Research

B elow are some of the main websites and channels you can use to conduct extended market research. Again let me emphasize here that it is very important to conduct thorough research before investing time and money. You may think it's a great idea but let the data prove that first. Then you can confidently go all in.

Google

Google is pretty much the boss of data these days. When it comes to marketing research Google trends is your best friend. The main point of Google trends is to reveal search behaviour of potential customers to business owners. This will help you to find answers to important questions during your market research phase. You will need to know:

- The search terms potential customers use
- Where search interest comes from
- Any related terms that are popular or rising in popularity
- How your brand ranks in comparison to competitors

Using Google Trends doesn't require a Google account. It's as simple as typing in the term you're looking to get more information on. Then you will be presented with it's trend data, related queries and interest by region. This will help you to gain a clearer understanding of your target audience. Plus you will gain more useful keywords, subtopics, trends and so on.

Google trends provides the popularity of a term over a period of time. The highest point of interest on the graph is one hundred and all other points are relative to that. For more accurate numbers you can use Google's Keyword Tool.

Google Keyword Tool

Find more search trends by using the free to use Google Keyword Tool. Simply head over to Google Keyword Tool and search for related keywords. Google will then present to you various related keywords along with how many monthly searches are performed for those related keywords. The data comes from Google searches which practically everyone uses these days.

Facebook

Facebook is another huge pool of data for you to draw from. Here you can access Facebook Audience Insights for Market Research. This will provide a wealth of data about your customer interest, purchasing behaviors and demographics. Plus all of that is free to use.

Facebook Audience Insights consists of compiled information from the platform and from other partners matched to user IDs on Facebook. Essentially this includes three different sets of people. All Facebook users, those linked to your Facebook page and users from a unique audience specified by you. A powerful benefit is that you can learn vital audience information and then use that to expand it by discovering more similar interest people. Plus by knowing your audience it will allow you to become better at creating more useful content and offers. This will in turn lead to better returns on investments on advertising spend and through campaigns.

Audience Insights on Facebook

The audience insights tool isn't actually that well known and can be difficult to find. To access it you need to go through your Adverts Manager account. For a new user this might be a bit complex at first. But don't worry, let's take a look at it together.

Step one: Select an audience - Audience Insights will begin by offering you to select from three options:
1. Everyone on Facebook
2. People connected to your page
3. A custom audience

Let's take a look at each option.

Option one: Everyone on Facebook. Select this if you're starting a new business and don't know much about your target customers.

Option two: People connected to your page. Select this if you would like to gain more knowledge about your existing audience and in turn develop new ideas for content that are useful to them.

Option three: A custom audience. Select this if you receive a decent amount of traffic to your domain, or you have a significant sized email list.

Step Two. Build a target audience. - On the left side panel of the audience insights area you can find a tab called "Create Audience". Then you can choose countries, regions and specific demographics of where your target audience resides. For best results start out with a broader region. Keep age and gender also broader during the initial testing phases.

Step three. Save the data - When researching different audiences it will help you later to define personas which can be used to guide your marketing. Use a spreadsheet to create and test customer personas. You can input various metrics which you can also add to later on. Beware that Facebook is always revising its data so be sure to keep it fresh.

Analyzing Facebook Audience Insights

There are six key categories that should be used.

1. Demographics - Use this to see the lifestyle data interests. This can be very helpful when marketing and planning for your target. For example if they lead a healthy life. Here you

can also see the relationship status, personas, qualifications, and career.

2. Page Likes - Here you can find information about any genre of pages they like on Facebook along with ten pages which they are probably to be interested in.

3. Location - Here you will be presented with details of the top locations of where audiences are likely to be found. Which can be useful when narrowing down your campaigns to specific regions.

4. Activity - Within this section there are two key things to consider. Frequency of activities and device users. This will display how active someone is on Facebook, and also the kind of activities that they are performing the most on Facebook. For example you can find out if they are receptive to advertising and how they

access Facebook. Such as through their phone, laptop or iPad and so on.

5. Household - In this section are valuable insights which share household income, ownership, market value, size and spending ways.

6. Purchase - This is probably the most important detail to consider, purchase behavior. Here you will find the most common purchasing habits of your audience. In addition you will find what kind of products they often buy.

With all of the above data, insights and research in mind you can start to try out new content based on it. Be sure to experiment with this because it's not going to work everytime. Some methods might provide better yield than others.

YouTube

YouTube is an extremely valuable resource that is often overlooked when conducting marketing research. Simply put, it's huge and you should not ignore it. With over two billion monthly users worldwide there is no denying its value. Plus it's very easy to learn about your audience and competition.

When you're starting out, get to know about YouTube demographics which present quantitative data. This includes where users live, age range and viewing preferences. These metrics will help you to create relevant and engaging content for your audience.

Sign up for a business YouTube channel and you will be given access to the Analytics tab. Use this tab to discover more about your YouTube audience. For example you can then monitor watch time and demographics. In addition check out any comments people leave on your videos. Again all of this will help you to craft the most engaging content.

Start researching your competition. YouTube is a highly competitive space. In order to identify opportunities and analyze how your channel measures up will require effective research. First of all, start identifying competitors. Select three to five. You can use Google Keyword Planner to identify companies that are ranking with similar keywords to your brand. Additionally you can search those keywords on YouTube and see what channels appear.

Take note of the number of subscribers and how many views they are getting. Those can serve as benchmarks for your channel. Analyze the titles and descriptions of their videos. Take note of what they say and the keywords they are using. In addition read the comments on the videos. This will give you insights into your potential target market.

Once you have some videos up and running on your channel it's time to track your results. What you measure grows. Success on YouTube requires testing and tracking. At least if it doesn't work then you learn from it. YouTube provides an excellent analytics tool to monitor how your channel is growing and the performance of your videos. In addition monitor the comments on your videos. Take note of what people are saying and also check out the community tab to see what people are talking about.

Instagram

Instagram is huge. Behind Facebook it is the second most accessed network in the world. According to Oberlo "almost seventy five percent of US businesses are on Instagram". With over one billion active monthly users it is for sure one to check out. Clearly Instagram has become more than for just personal use. It can now be used to reach a global audience for brands. Every month users engage and shop there. For a brand it is essential!

The advantage of Instagram as a way of marketing and branding is that it is visual. For businesses that feature strong designs as their advantage then it is a great platform to showcase that on. Videos, photography and art are all excellent fits for Instagram. However first of all you will need to have a well defined strategy before you just start posting content.

Before you post anything, define why your brand is on Instagram. It shouldn't be just because it is a popular platform. In order to be successful there you will need purpose and goals to justify your efforts and investments. Reasons could be anything from selling products to showcasing features. Or maybe you just want to grow your audience globally. Make a list of what your reasons are to help and guide you.

Moving forwards determine who your target audience will be. Instagram offers highly targeted advertising which allows you to target metrics such as age, demographic, gender, interests and so on. Try to build a detailed profile for your target audience. If you struggle here then conduct market research first on Instagram. Take note of the popular events, locations and hashtags that are related to your brand. The discover tab is a great way to do this. Engage with similar content to your brand and follow those pages. Eventually the algorithm will start to present you with more relevant content that you can then use in your market research.

Take a look at your potential competitors. Note what they post. Note how often they post. Note their style of posts. Find out what their highest engaging posts are. Build an idea of what to aim for. Look at ways you can improve on that and be a little different. Take note of any potential missed opportunities.

When you have a clearer idea of what your position will be and the kind of content you will be posting you can start to curate a plan of forthcoming content. Create an editorial calendar that can be filled with all your forthcoming posts, captions, times, hashtags and so on. Success on Instagram comes from carefully curated content. In addition you will need to analyze what works and what does not. Take note of your posts that have great engagement and try to make more like those.

Focus long term on building a brand that consistently delivers its promises and values. Continue to grow your followers. Don't try to take shortcuts and buy followers. It looks fake and could get you banned. Plus those followers won't engage with your content. Instead go about doing it the real way. Sure this will take time and effort but in the end it will all be worthwhile.

First of all, make yourself easy to be found and followed. Make sure your username is easy to search and representative of your brand. Don't use a bunch of weird spellings or special characters. If people struggle to find you then they won't follow you. Fill in your bio section. Include what it is your brand does and what it promises to its followers. Bring awareness to you. Follow similar accounts to yours and engage in a natural way with their posts. Comment on them but don't be spammy. Make use of promotions and deals to drive more engagement and followers. Contests are also great for this.

Use Instagram Stories to get customer feedback

Instagram stories are highly engaging and a great way to get direct customer feedback. One of the most effective ways to understand your customers is to use polls on the stories. The poll sticker is an easy and effective way of understanding your customers. It will allow you to shar polls on your stories which customers can share their feedback on. Use fields such as "yes" and "no" for discovering brand ideas.

In addition, make full use of Instagram direct messaging to communicate with businesses and consumers. Brand interaction in this way is excellent for establishing personal connections. Great for brand loyalty.

Amazon

Amazon has almost fifty percent of the US retail market share. With a constantly growing revenue and overtaking of traditional commerce it is for sure a marketplace that should be utilized when it comes to branding and market research. Almost every kind of product is on there so again it makes sense to utilize it.

Conducting market research on Amazon is both free and easy to do. There are some paid tools you can use but those are usually more specific to a particular type of product. To conduct research use Google Chrome and install Amazon BSR chrome extension. This is a free extension and it will show you the average best seller rank of any product on Amazon. Once it is installed the data will just show up whenever you're on Amazon.

Conducting research for new product ideas utilizes the Amazon best seller rank to see what's selling and how competitive it is. These metrics will help you to identify high demand and low competition products.

Step one: Search Google for "Amazon best sellers" this will present you lists of all the best sellers on Amazon. Click the official Amazon link. It should be the first link.

Step two: On the left hand column you will be presented with a bunch of categories. Let's say for example you're interested in the wellness niche. Click the relevant category. On the next page you can then narrow it down even more using the subcategories.

Step three: Now you should have a page of ranked results. Create an excel sheet with columns including products, number of reviews, rank and price.

Step four: Start recording data on products you think are relevant to your niche. You can get a good idea of price points, competition and so on. For example if there are lots of products with many reviews then it might be a bit competitive.

Or maybe you can see how you could do it better. Use the results to your advantage.

If you're looking for quicker ways to do market research on Amazon consider some great paid tools such as Kdspy, Bookbeam and KDP Rocket.

Part Three: Unique Branding Strategies Top Brands Use To Thrive

Brand Strategy

Successful brands are established through setting clear goals which translate into a clear long term brand strategy. A great brand strategy can help make a brand stand out from the average ones. There are some key guidelines that are involved in successfully setting brand goals. Number one there has to be a good reason behind every action associated with a brand. Consider what you are trying to achieve. It needs to be clear what the aims are. If this is not clear then time and money will be wasted. Plus growth will not happen. With clear goals and strategy it's much easier to make sense of every action towards progress. When it comes to strategy and standing out there are a number of important brand goals to consider.

The goal of brand awareness is to increase how well a brand is known. Essentially it is about reaching the most amount of people possible. This is the most important goal. Once you have that differentiating factor you need to present brand awareness as far and as wide as possible. Without awareness no one knows about the brand and ultimately of course no one will buy from it. How well known do you want to be? How many followers do you want? What kind of ranking do you wish to achieve? Such goals require understanding target audiences, markets, having a great online presence and making sure the brand stands out.

Clearly if people don't see your brand in the first place then it won't last. The only way to get the ball rolling is to be as visible as possible. That means at the start spreading the word far and wide. Experiment with different marketing and social media platforms. Experiment with advertising and testing out different content. Experiment with different formats and mediums. Find what drives the most traffic and go all in on it. Make sure your social media and SEO is on point. Spread it out there, be visible and get noticed. Spread your content across multiple channels.

Emotional connection

The goal of creating an emotional connection is to resonate with target audiences which in turn will influence sales and loyalty. Stories about why the company was started or its values and ethics are great ways of creating emotional connections. They should be told with passion, meaning and be relatable. The brand Gym Shark has a great emotional connection with its customers because the story of its founder is well known. CEO Ben Francis started out in his parents house sewing the garments after working his shift as a pizza delivery boy.

Every brand should strive to create and maintain relationships with customers. This can be done by targeting their needs. Additionally, focus on your brand's reputation. Choose the right strategies and ambassadors to uphold the brand.

Be Unique

The goal of uniqueness is to find out what separates your brand from the competition. Perhaps that is quality, price or value. Whatever it is, promote it through your content. Make sure your customers know what is unique about your brand. Be clear about it and define it. Keep it simple. Standing out in a crowded market depends on this. Consider offering competitive prices, offer relevant products or services and ultimately offer great value.

Attempting to copy another brand is a bad idea. No, focus on creating an original brand! Try to come up with a new angle or a new solution to an old problem and be original. It might take time to create that uniqueness but it's worth it. Originality is what will set your brand apart from the rest. Specific differentiators are dependent on the type of brand. For example some brands can be different by utilizing shape. Or some might utilize color and words. You get the idea. Think about why you purchase some brands over others. Imagine going into a store and buying your brand. What would make it stand out?

Be Real

Public perception of a brand is vital to its success. The public needs to perceive that the brand is sincere. It is therefore the responsibility of the brand to be real. One way that can be conveyed is through its interactions with customers. Instead of talking formally or copy pasting responses, speak to them as a friend would. If your brand makes mistakes then be honest about it. Your customers will appreciate that.

The goal is to win potential clients and maintain loyalty with existing ones. For small brands this is much more important. In most cases having an online presence is the best way to build trust. Make sure customers can easily give feedback, even if it is negative. Take it all as being a way to improve. Reply to their concerns. In fact, do it publicly. Social media makes it possible for brands to present their personality which allows consumers to engage with them. This makes things much more transparent and much easier to trust.

Be Bold

It's better to risk being offended than staying neutral and being forgotten. Sometimes a brand has to take a risk. They have to be bold and experiment. That could come from trying new techniques, taking a controversial stance or cementing a new partnership. Any of these could be polarizing and potentially alienate some of the market. But at the same time it could trigger a viral reaction. Remember you don't want to be forgotten as just another brand so be bold, take a risk and stand out.

Be Valuable

Ultimately brands need to offer value to their customers. That value needs to be more than what is offered by its competitors. How can a brand offer more value? Well it needs to think about offering better products or services. That could be based on time, quality, price or other variables. Research what's important to the customer. Research the weaknesses of the competitors and what customers say about them. Craft your value incentive around research.

Keep offering value as needs and markets change. Imagine your brand is the best friend of the consumer. It makes sense to be real and relatable like this. Think about when you met your best friend. It was because you shared mutual interests and vibes. Try to relate to your consumers in the same way. Talk about what interests them and go with their vibe.

The most successful brands understand their target markets. They demonstrate this through compassionate branding. In effect they recognize the pain points of the target audience and provide solutions. This creates more trust and loyalty from the customers. Be sure to constantly communicate with your audience and work on understanding them more.

Be Engaging

Create a narrative around your brand. Storytelling is a powerful tactic used in marketing brands. For the audience it gives them something to connect with. Be engaging and weave this narrative into all of your brand from its marketing to its content and so on. We will explore this in more detail later on. For now realize that storytelling is highly engaging and will help your brand stand out.

Purchasing

The goal of purchasing is to create more sales. This is achieved through motivating customers to buy services or products. Incentivize them with great offers and extra reasons to buy. Trigger them with strategies that drive purchases. Sales funnels and lead generation tactics work well here. Additionally work on effective advertising campaigns, new deals and make use of endorsements.

The above points will help to start building a brand and to help it stand out. If you already have a brand, consider reflecting on those points and how your brand stands up to them. Be open to making changes.

Pricing Strategies

Pricing is often the first step to competing. But choosing a price can require a long thought out process with some trial and error. If prices are too high you could scare off customers. But price them too low and you might lose valuable profits or worse be seen as low quality. The good news is that there are a number of pricing strategies available to help you to decide on the right prices. Those cover being a suitable price for your audience whilst also helping you to achieve revenue goals.

Price will determine whether your brand is a need or a luxury. However with the right message you can communicate if it is matching the customers needs and desires. In other words if it's worth the price tag. Knowing your audience is paramount here. First of all you need to know if it is affordable to them. If it is a stretch for them then you will need to give them some solid reasons to buy. That could be for example high quality, longevity or status.

The basic rule of pricing is that it must match what the customers value it to be whilst also being profitable enough to the brand. Consumers will usually compare the price of one brand with another. They will consider competitor pieces and experiences. That creates a frame of reference for them. If a brand and its price does not fit well into that comparison then it will struggle to sell. It's not just about the cost of something, it's also about the value of it. Think about it, if cost were the only factor then we would only buy the cheapest services and products. As you will see there is a considerable amount of thought that goes into purchasing decisions. The amount of money a consumer is willing to pay has much more to do with their value perception. Successful brands need to determine the value of their products and services for their target audience. That begins with a pricing analysis.

Pricing Analysis

Pricing strategies begin with pricing analysis which is the evaluation of your pricing strategy against market demands. The goal is to identify how price changes can lead to better opportunities. Those would be improved revenues and customer satisfaction.

The most effective method is to run tests. Pricing strategies need to test out the waters and see how they place in the market. This should also be checked again at least once a year. Such preemptive checks will help to avoid losses in business. To begin with, calculate the costs of your products or services. Make a note of all expenses both fixed and variable that go into such products or services. With those identified, subtract them from a price estimate. A price estimate can be decided upon by researching the market. Conduct focus groups, questionnaires and so on to the target market. In addition, make a note of the competitors prices. Those should be competitors who sell exactly the same thing or something comparable. Next launch it and see how sales are. If the sales are not so good then consider lowering the price or choosing a better strategy.

Pricing Strategy

A pricing strategy can be thought of as the method used to decide on the best price of a service or product. Again, ideally it should be a balance between being the most profitable to a brand whilst also offering the most value to consumers. There are a number of key influences towards a pricing strategy. Mainly those are revenue goals, competition, economic trends and demand. Choosing a price is one of the most important parts of marketing a brand. Now of course it won't satisfy all consumers. Some may be turned off by a price point whilst it may attract others. However ideally it should attract more. Here are some strategies to consider.

Value-Based Pricing strategy

The Value-Based Pricing strategy focuses on what the customer will gain in value from using a product or service. Costs are not part of the equaliuton. This works well for brands that are quite unique. For example iPhones are not that expensive to make yet their prices are quite high. Some would indeed say they are overpriced. However, it's the value they offer to customers that determines their price. To its loyal customers they are unique and add significant value to them.

Competition Pricing Strategy

A competition pricing strategy defines price by determining the going market rate for a particular product or service. Costs and demand are not factored into the equation. Rather the benchmark is set by competitor prices. This type of strategy is most effective in saturated markets. For example when people buy general food such as milk or rice they tend to focus on price. Since there are so many options, price is the clearest way to stand out. Consumers will be looking for value for money. In this type of situation brands can compete by pricing slightly lower than their competitors. Later they could raise it.

Cost-Plus Pricing Strategy

In a cost plus pricing strategy brands set their prices based on how much they would like to profit. To apply this strategy a fixed percentage of cost for a product or service should be added on the top. For example, say it costs $20 to make a hat and you wish to profit $20 per sale then your price would be $40. That is a markup of one hundred percent.

Cost plus pricing strategies tend to work best with physical products where margins and costs are easier to identify. However brands should not become too greedy because inevitably if they seek too much profit then they may price themselves out of the market.

Dynamic Pricing Strategy

A dynamic pricing strategy is a more flexible pricing strategy. According to customer demand and the market, prices will fluctuate. Events, hotels, flights and so on are mostly using this strategy. Through application of algorithms it allows them to shift prices as market trends and demands change. Nowadays these algorithms have become very sophisticated and can even estimate when a customer is ready to purchase. Prices will fluctuate according to how often and when the customer visits the quote page.

Freemium Pricing Strategy

When a brand offers a basic or trial version of their product it is a freemium pricing strategy. Usually customers will become comfortable and happy with a product or service. After a trial period or to get full features they would usually upgrade. It's a great way to open the door and let people in slowly. Prices should not jump too much from a free price though. Usually smaller monthly payments would provide the best customer acquisition. At the initial stages this can be costly so brands need to prepare in advance. However in the long run with automatic payments and so on it can become very lucrative.

Offering your products or services for free allows customers to get a feel of your brand before they commit to purchasing. At the beginning this is great to get the ball rolling. Plus there are ways that can still make this profitable for your brand. For example you can offer a seven day free trial period. After which most will probably sign up for the paid plan. Or if suitable you could use watermarks on free versions so if your customers use your products then there is some advertising. Which is great because it's more brand awareness for you.

Discount pricing strategy

The discount pricing strategy begins with a brand selling at a high price and when demand goes down so does the price. You probably have seen examples of this in discounts, sales, clearances, last chance buys and so on. Primarily this is utilized by retailers to sell off remaining stocks from last season. Particularly for products that are seasonal or change often such as fashion. Consumers are very receptive to this strategy and anticipate such special days coming up. In addition brands can also consider bundling or give buy one get one free and so on. This is another great way to add value to customers and essentially get them to buy more.

Hourly Pricing Strategy

Freelancers, consultants and contractors providing business services typically start out by basing their services on an hourly pricing strategy. Essentially it trades time for money. As you can imagine this is limited in how much someone can earn and it becomes difficult to scale on an individual level. However for short projects and contracts it can make sense. In some situations a very lucrative price can be set. That price of course depends on quality of service and demand. Alternatively a project based pricing strategy could be implemented. This would instead require a flat fee for a project. Suich a price can be estimated based on value, time required, base rate costs and demand.

Penetration Pricing Strategy

When a brand enters a new market it is going to be difficult to break through. This is when a penetration pricing strategy comes in useful. The strategy works by entering the market at a low price that draws attention away from comptrits. However this will usually be at a loss so it is not sustainable. Apply this for a short time and it can help to acquire new customers. Then they will ideally be happy with the services and products and when it comes time to increase prices they will be comfortable.

Premium Pricing Strategy

For more luxury brands a premium pricing strategy helps them to present an image of luxury and high value status. Consumers usually associate higher prices with higher quality. Brands should only charge a premium price if their products and services are in fact premium. Otherwise it will lead to bad reputation and loss of business. Brands in fashion and automobiles for example are often using this strategy. It helps to market them as exclusive and luxury.

Psychological Pricing Strategy

It's well known that sales can be boosted using psychological tactics. One of the most well known psychological tactics is to price a product with the "9" in the price. When people see something at for example $49.99 it doesn't seem so expensive. Essentially it's $50 but use of a "9" makes it seem like a better deal.

Another psychological tactic is to place expensive items next to something you wish to sell. That makes it look like a great deal. Gym memberships for example make good use of this. They would put a fairly expensive daily rate next to a more valuable monthly rate. Additional psychological tactics can be to adjust font sizes and colors of pricing information. These adjustments can help to boost sales. When you understand the target market more you can directly target their psychological make up.

To conclude, remember that pricing is something that can change and shift with trends and so on. It's not something that should be set in stone forever.

Standing Out!

E very market place is a crowded one. In recent times it has become even more difficult to stand out. Consumers are faced with unlimited choices. There's no escaping the fact that there are an overwhelming amount of competitors out there. All brands are competing for vivisitibily. Target audiences are overwhelmed with advertising and marketing. But brands that succeed are aware of that and work to get the edge over their competition. Unfortunately there is not one single tactic to beat the competition. Incidentally it relies on the combination of many factors.

Naturally gaining consumer attention in such a saturated market is difficult. That's why building an established and recognized brand is important. Advertising alone isn't going to be enough. Your brand needs to stand out and be remembered by consumers. When their needs arise the brand that stands out will be what springs up in their memory. In fact, being memorable is incremental towards brand success. First of all it builds trust. Once a consumer is more aware of a brand they begin to trust it. When consumers trust something they are much more likely to buy from it. With brand awareness that trust is established. Plus it helps to give the brand personality and establish a relationship with their customers.

Think about it like this. When you want to find something out, what do you do? You probably search Google for it. Say for example, you want to eat ice cream, what do you do? Well you probably go eat that tub of Ben & Jerrys or whatever your favourite ice cream brand is. Those decisions are made because you're aware of that brand and that is the power of brand awareness. Actions become associated with particular products or services from brands.

So how can a brand stand out?

First of all the goal is to make customers perceive the brand in a particular way. A brand that stands out from the competition has a strong identity. Just think of any big brand and you will instantly recognize it along with having certain associations to it. A strong brand identity doesn't happen overnight. It's about making the right choices through trial, error and research. Standing by those choices helps to build trust and familiarity. Therefore brands need to plan for the long term.

Customers tend to favour the brands that they have had a positive experience with. That can be conveyed through the brand identity and how it is relayed consistently to customers. This is known as the "halo effect" which correlates with brand strength and customer loyalty. When customers begin to have a preference towards a certain brand it is because that brand has a strong identity.

Without a strong identity brands will not be so successful. Worst case scenarios can create a horn effect which is the opposite of the halo effect. Just imagine the devil's horns. It correlates with a negative experience associated with a brand. A small weakness in a brand can create negative associations. Therefore brands need to present a fully positive reputation. For example a weak online presence may negatively affect the brands overall reputation.

Successful brands take into account the whole picture of the brand and make sure it is consistent. Everything a brand does affects the perception and reputation of it. A poor design, weak identity, bad reputation and poor communication can hurt the brand. That's why it's good practice to work on building and shaping a brand. All of it adds up which then helps to build trust and credibility. Leaving it to chance is not a good strategy. The brands that stand out take the management of their brand seriously. Managing all components of a brand is paramount because if any part is neglected then its influence on customers is weakened. Smart and intentional choices are required here.

Purpose

A strong brand will effectively communicate its purpose, what it does and how it does it. Furthermore, strong brands that stand out are effective at establishing trust and credibility with their customers and prospects. The process of branding has the goal to build awareness and loyalty though a strong brand image. A great example of a strong brand identity is the McDonald's arches. The Golden Arches are one of the most recognizable symbols in branding. The original intent behind the design was to be visible and noticed over long distances. This worked well with the drive in concept and for passers by. Furthermore such a simple logo can be recognized by children who incidentally are a target audience of the restaurant. Children can in turn have an influence on their parents stopping to eat there.

Another example of a strong brand identity would be the fashion brand Gucci. The literal meaning of the word Gucci is to represent fashion, excellence and greatness. The logo uses two G's which represent the initials of the man who started it, Guccio Gucci. Gold colors are mostly used with the logo. Such colors are associated with luxury and high society. Strong identity is shown through the Gucci name being clearly spelled out above the emblem.

Over the years the Gucci brand has become world famous. For those interested in luxury fashion it is instantly recognizable. Appearing on the most fashionable pieces of clothing, being supported by models, celebrities and so on has helped its fame. For the rich and famous it proves their wealth and as such it is seen as a status symbol by those who wear it. Such positive associations make it a very powerful and strong brand.

Naturally when a consumer becomes more aware of a brand then they almost subconsciously make purchasing decisions. This is why top brands such as Coca Cola spread their logos everywhere. More and more recognition equals more trust and yes buying influence. It just keeps spreading on and on. Eventually it travels by word of mouth and then soon enough a brand becomes a household name. Now this won't happen overnight or from one single marketing campaign. Building brand awareness requires multiple strategic efforts. Below you will find some useful ways to help you establish brand awareness.

Define Unique Selling Points (USP)

Unless you're the only player in your market you will need to differentiate yourself from your competitors. That requires defining your unique selling proposition, or USP. Having a strong and recognizable USP is what makes or breaks businesses. This means it is essential to long term success.

USPs are what make your brand different from the competition. These should be focused on what benefits the customers and the qualities that add the most value to them. Again you need to know exactly who your customers are. Use the earlier chapter to help you get clear on that. Be clear and concise about them since they will become key elements of your brand.

Identifying your USP can be achieved by addressing specific needs of the brands target audience. Here are some examples.

FedEx

"When it absolutely, positively has to be there overnight."

When FedEx was first starting out they used this slogan. As a delivery service this is an excellent proposition of value to its customers. Those target customers of the brand want exactly that. The USP is perfectly articulated in their slogan.

Domino Pizza

"We deliver hot, fresh pizza in 30 minutes or less or it's free."

Here is a really cool example of understanding the pain points of a customer. We all have experienced waiting too long for a food delivery. Or worse it arrives cold. Domino verbalizes this pain point and makes a promise not to happen. Best of all if it does you get it free. There is a great USP encapsulated.

The North Face

"Products that last a lifetime"

The North Face is a clothing company specializing in outdoor activities such as climbing, caving and exploring. In these scenarios long lasting products are essential. That very promise is made in the USP of The North Face. Incidentally this helps it to stand out from the others since this is a pain point of its target market. It also makes a promise to establish trust in the brand.

USP Best Practices

With the above examples in mind you should have a better idea of what a USP entails. Now let's work on creating a USP. First of all work on understanding the mindset of your perfect customer. That means knowing exactly who you need to target and why. Then you can consider the following:

- What do they really want?
- What are the problems you can solve for them?
- What motivates them to buy?
- Why choose you?

Answers to these questions will start to paint a picture of your USP. Once you know who your perfect customer is and the problems they have then you can begin to explain why they should choose your brand. That could be about making a promise. Such as Fedex promising it to be there overnight. Are there any promises to solve customer pain points that you can offer?

Alternatively you can think of your USP like an elevator pitch. That is it should quickly capture attention and explain the value. Just like an advert you have only a few seconds to capture their attention. Therefore the USP should be instantly clear. Incidentally that will pay off in advertising campaigns. Highlight the USP in any advertising copy. It could even be the headline. Emphasize the benefits of the brand and deliver value.

Even more ways to stand out

Sponsor events

There are literally millions of festivals, exhibitions, seminars, concerts and events out there. You will always see tons of brands sponsoring events. Again it's about building brand awareness. Many people attend these events, film them, share them and so on. If your brand is in the mix then it's a good exposure of getting your brand in front of more people. Find relevant events to your brand. Then at the very least get your brand logos on some products, banners or wherever you can.

Guest blog

Brands should all have blogs primed for their audience. Additionally they can guest blog for other publications. Start searching your keywords to find similar blogs. Many sites will welcome guest posts. Check the site's content to be sure it is a great fit for you. Come up with some engaging content that fits in with them. It should add value to both of you. Value to you through exposure and value to them through new perspectives.

Infographics

Infographics are one of the most shared types of content. They are great for reaching new audiences and have the potential to go viral. Usually these are very engaging and easy to consume. You can quickly summarize a regular article into something much easier and more fun to digest.

Search engine optimization (SEO)

To many of us, SEO looks a little overwhelming. However nowadays tech giants have made it easy to implement. A website or page with great SEO will place you optimally on Google search results. To begin, find relevant keywords for your brand. Focus on what people would search for exactly when trying to find your brand. Make use of tools such as SEMrush, Google Keyword tool and Moz Keyword Researcher to discover the most important keywords. Create content based on those keywords. If some keywords have low competition and high demand plus they are highly relevant to your brand then go all in on them. Keep track of the results and adjust as necessary.

Referrals

One of the best brand awareness strategies is referrals. When people hear about you via word of mouth it is certified as trusted and as such results in high conversions. Many people find out about brands through friends and family. In addition there are various referral programs out there which work by offering incentives, promotions, discounts and so on for when people refer a friend. For brand and customer it's a win-win situation. Start searching for referral programs within your niche. Ask people to share your message.

Social media

An important part of brand awareness is social media. Now more than ever social media is the most powerful source of traffic. People are spending time there all day. Keep updating and creating content on your social media. Make sure it is high quality and relevant. Be consistent in your posting. Keep going every week. Tag customers, share stories and engage. Make use of events, competitions and tools to drive engagement and following.

Podcast

In recent times podcasts have become more and more popular. People tune into them regularly and form a dedicated group of followers. Now you don't necessarily need to start a podcast. Being a guest on one can get you going. Or if you do start one then gaining traffic can be achieved through having well known guests on your show. Consider all the podcasts and guests possible in your niche.

Collaboration

All markets are pretty saturated right now. But that doesn't mean that you can't stand out. Why not stand on the shoulders of another brand? Discover similar minded brands who want to raise awareness through collaboration. Maybe you could team your t-shirt brand with a shoe brand for some limited edition products. Or team up your coffee brand with a bagel shop. You get the idea. Find some excellent partnerships and increase brand awareness through collaboration.

Influencers are also great to connect with. Maybe you're struggling with connecting to your market. This is where influencers can come in handy. These are the people with an established fan base in your market. Connect with them to start sharing your content with their audience. Connecting with popular brands and personalities in your niche will help you to reach a wider audience. You can even leverage influencers to create content for you. They will understand what works for their audience. By collaborating with them you will receive great content specifically for your audience. Plus you will gain more recognition.

How to reach out to collaborators

The first question you should always ask before you pitch to any potential partner is, will they sell my product? It's smart advice not to waste their or your time on potential mismatches. However if you have identified a great fit then start to map out and list the ways that you could collaborate. Highlight the benefits it will bring to them. You can mention metrics such as your reach, fanbase, previous collaborations and anything else of potential value. Or highlight the incentives you will give them. Financial or rewards and so on.

In addition you will need to be clear on what it is you want to promote and why. Be honest and direct about this. The better the clarity of understating between your collaborations the better the relationship will be. Be sure to mention all of this in your pitch.

143

To help you with reaching out to potential collaborators here is a template for you to use.

"Hey (their name),

I'm a big fan of (their product) and would love to share details about it with my (number of) followers. Let me know if you're interested?

Here is my (best social media link) and (anything else that is relevant)

It would be great to (propose how you plan to collaborate - eg, shares, affiliate, etc)

*here you can also include any people or brands you have collaborated with before.

Thanks,

(your name)"

Advertising

Advertising is one of the most effective brand awareness strategies out there. Most people won't be willing to invest into advertising. But don't be one of them. The fact is you won't need a pot of money to do it. Just be sensible and don't overspend. There are some low cost keywords and advertising strategies out there which will still ensure you get conversions and awareness. Make use of advertising on Google and social media as a primary method.

Advertising metrics and methods go beyond the scope of this book. But what I would recommend is to find low cost and high demand keywords. Niching down is a great way to do this. Plus be sure to learn as much about advertising as possible. It is an evolving industry so you will need to monitor it and keep upto date with developments.

Leads

A lead generation strategy is a way of attracting new customers whilst also capturing the information of potential new customers. The concept works through sending visitors to a landing page. Contact information is collected and then an automated system of converting them into sales is implemented. The success of capturing information relies on having an effective call to action or offer in exchange for contact information. This should be perceived as of value to the target market which will make it highly effective.

When starting out a brand's main goal is to attract as many new customers as possible. That means sending as many leads as possible to the landing page and then making sure as many as possible convert into paying customers. The main objective of the campaign will be to increase exposure for the brand. This is achieved through generating as many impressions for visits to the landing page as possible. The landing page is a specific web page with a call to action.

Staying Relevant

In addition to brand awareness brands need to stay relevant. Once they have achieved some awareness it can be difficult to maintain. Modern markets are changing all the time and customers' expectations are going up. The markets shift and trends emerge. Maintaining their position in the market and staying relevant is a daily struggle for brands.

To stay relevant brands need to constantly evolve with the times. They need to keep ahead of the competition and preempt customer expectations. This requires adaptation to customer needs and market changes. In some situations brands will have to reposition in order to stay relevant. For instance just look at how smoking brands have evolved. They used to be cool, trendy, and fashionable. However as people became aware of the serious health implications and government restrictions on advertising they evolved. To adapt they branded in places such as bars, pubs and events where smokers would tend to frequent. Another great example is how sports shoes became more fashionable. Previously they were associated with athletes. Nowadays many sports brands have expanded their reach and connected with music artists who have huge untapped markets of loyal customers.

Incidentally it's important to not just jump on a bandwagon for short term profits. This will be seen as fake to customers. Trends should only be incorporated if they match up with a brand and the values it stands by. Brands can still stay up with trends by innovating what they do. Just be original.

Always stay focused on the customer. Everything should be designed to meet the needs of the customer. Naturally those needs change so great brands should have a finger on the pulse of the market and its trends. Get into your customers' heads, analyze their decisions, lifestyles and so on. Stay relevant. Brand relevance requires maintaining trust and loyalty from customers. That can be achieved by being valuable and listening to them.

What Makes Content Go Viral?

E very single day an infinite amount of images, articles, blogs and posts are uploaded online. Almost all of them remain relatively unknown. But then there are the select few which go viral and explode across the internet. In a very short space of time they attract hundreds of thousands to some millions of hits. In some cases some content becomes so viral that it becomes a part of the public consciousness. The question is what makes such content go viral? Well there are many reasons. First of all, once a piece of content is posted the more engagement it gets the more it grows. This begins in smaller ecosystems such as between groups of friends. When the content breaks out of the small groups it then heads towards becoming mainstream.

Smart phones are owned by more than half of the population of most first world countries. It's never been easier to engage with content. Everyday we see news feeds just full of content. Typically these news feeds are ecosystems for generating the most viral content. Algorithms of the news feeds will place the most viral content at the top of the feed. Then it grows much quicker. As a brand you're going to be producing content, so get in the know.

Emotions count

Emotional content tends to go more viral. When emotions such as laughter or awe are triggered it connects us more with the content. Creators of content are well aware of this and as such carefully curate highly emotional content. Visuals in particular are highly effective at helping people to communicate emotions. For example memes are often exceptionally viral because they can effectively summarize someone's emotions. Stating such emotions in text is much more difficult and dry. In addition people are quickly stimulated by fast moving content in this modern world. Consider some of the most shareable emotions;

- Awe, happiness, pride, excitement, sadness, inspiration, joy, empathy

One of the most common reasons for people sharing content is to make others laugh. In addition primal emotions also influence how viral content will be. These emotions are innate triggers to humans. They include;

- Sexual arousal, fear, anger, fury, terror

How well emotions are connected with content is often what makes the content more appealing. Viral posts typically are not that confusing. Instantly they arouse an emotional state. Emotions are key drivers of why people share and purchase things. How much we care about something influences how prepared we are to share it. Most people have deep emotional connections with particular brands and services. Think about it. Do you use certain technology manufacturers? Or do you only eat at certain restaurants? I think you will likely realize that you're affected by this for your own individual reasons.

Usefulness

Perhaps one of the main reasons for something going viral is simply because it is useful. When an article, information, product or service is deemed to be very useful then naturally people will want to share it. Perhaps you share a news article that is motivational. Or a product to help your friend out.

Triggers

Anytime you hear a certain word it can cause you to think of a particular memory. This is known as a trigger and it is a powerful influence on the subconscious mind. For example, maybe you hear the word "fresh coffee" and you imagine sipping on warm fresh coffee. All of this is triggered by a simple word. Brands are well aware of such triggers and carefully use them in their marketing campaigns to drive sales. For example, "mind blowing" is often used in a variety of places. Many people use that phrase to describe a positive experience and so the association with a brand is very powerful indeed.

Social Triggers

Alongside emotions social triggers help make content go viral. People tend to share content because they believe it will make themselves look good to their friends, family and followers. This makes them feel valuable and look cool. Consider these examples of social triggers;

- Wanting to look good
- Sharing interested or passions
- Starting conversations
- Stating opinions
- Emotions

Remarkability

When content is worthy of attention it is remarkable. Advertisers know this. Lists are also a great way of making content go viral.

Viral content example: Psy Gangnam Style

In 2012 South Korean pop star Psy released the video for his new song "Gangnam Style". Subsequently it went viral and spread like a wildfire. By late 2013 it had quickly become the most viewed video ever in YouTube history with over 1.8 billion views. How did this happen?

Behind the scenes there were some carefully laid plans to the viral success of the video. YG Entertainment, the record label which Psy was signed to had recently made significant moves to push their artists worldwide. Deals with The UK and The US music industry executives helped to set the stage for a viral hit. The company also invested in growing a highly engaged audience on their platforms. This would ensure maximum exposure for the song when it was released. Pre-release they already had a combined 2.5 million users across their channels. In addition they had an excellent network of highly engaged and mass followed Twitter accounts to spread and share. This foundation of seeding accounts and platforms were key components to the success. From day one the video would reach many views. Lesson, have an engaged and dense platform to launch content on.

Now having a big stage to launch on is one thing. But if your content sucks then it will simply not get shared and it will disappear into obscurity with all the other content out there. So what made "Gangnam Style" so shareable? Since it was a foreign language song you might think that would be a global barrier. However the song featured easy to understand lyrics and a catchy chorus. The video for it was visually bright and colorful which is very attractive for kids. In addition the video featured well known South Korean entertainers which combined with the already popular Psy made it more shareable. Key success in this was tweets from popular twitter accounts. Trend setters on YouTube and Twitter picked up on this. More people shared it. Then it kept on growing. Remember if you follow certain people then you're more emotionally connected with them and then more likely to share their content. Lesson, have a solid platform and create connections with your audience. Treat them like your friends. Also working with influencers in your content is great to make it more shareable.

Part Four: Driving Brand Loyalty With Emotion… Think Human Experience!

Brand Journey & Psychology

Stories are a powerful way of building emotional connections because humans are deeply affected by them. In the past brands relied more on marketing and advertising to influence their success. Nowadays with the prominence of online reputations and awareness creating a brand story is more important. It is also much easier to achieve. Consumers love to feel like their purchases are relevant to their lifestyle and beliefs. Brands that use cold hard marketing tactics might find it difficult to be relatable. Those brands that connect with the values of their consumers are great at being relatable. For example Tesla focuses on clean energy which is a significant concern of their target market.

Having a journey behind a brand is an essential component to its success. It serves to convey the brand's perception in the public eye. Creating a powerful brand story relies on getting to the meaning and motivation of the brand. In order to establish trust with customers, time and effort needs to be spent on carefully constructing a brand story.

When customers make purchases it is either because of a need or a want. Maybe they need it for everyday life or they are wanting to add value to their life. When making those purchases they will look for certain qualities. Brands that can convey those qualities are the ones who succeed. Trust and belief is installed in them and that in turn drives purchases.

A brand that can demonstrate its values through its story helps it to be more personable and display the qualities which customers are likely to be seeking. Without such a story customers are less likely to resonate with a brand or ultimately purchase from it. Storytelling is how a brand can drive a purpose and make an impact. With a compelling story it will drive business decisions and at the end sales.

Define a brand journey

Start by defining the brand journey. A great brand journey presents all the facts and information about the brand. Make it compelling. It should evoke positive emotions with the audience and forge a connection with them. In turn this will drive customer loyalty. A brand story is the very foundation of a brand. Through its story a powerful force of recognition is established. This is what customers will come to trust. Consider some of the following questions.

- Does the brand feature a strong narrative across all channels?
- Does the brand have an origin story?
- Does the brand have a clear mission?
- How does the brand add value to its customers?
- Does the brand have clear values and personality traits?

Let's now take a look at steps to creating a brand story.

Brand Statement

The brand statement is the first and most important step of curating a brand story. The meaning and mission of the brand should be conveyed here. This will help people to understand what the brand is about. It should answer the questions of what it is about and why it is about in the first place.

Back Story

Begin the brand journey with details about how the business was started and where it plans to go in the future. Share the struggles and the obstacles along the way. Take them on a journey. Customers can trust a brand if it is more real. An authentic backstory and goals make this more plausible. Highlight the reasons for starting the business. Include any points of interest that could create a personal bond with the consumer.

How a business got going and the struggles of starting out is a great connection point with consumers. This can personalize a brand and present it as being more human. How and why was the brand started? Of course money is often a big motivation but beyond that what passions influenced the start?

Have a beginning, middle and end to your story. Where was it started? Where is it now?

Where is it going? Spare no details and write it as a historical account. Include all the interesting parts, the trials and errors. Move onto detailing the purpose and dreams behind the foundation. Highlight what the purpose of the brand is. State why it now exists. Be creative and make a statement. Ask why it is here? Be true and authentic.

Focus on talking about the personal elements such as the goals and mission. Demonstrate the brand values and integrate them into the story. Focus on why they are important. Keep it simple and relatable. Brand stories should quickly grab the audience's attention and get them invested. That is possible by understanding the audience.

In previous chapters you will have used the methods to gather important audience information. Focus on that demographic, what motivates them and what they like and dislike.

Base the brand story on the audience's interests. Appeal to them but do it in a way that correlates with your brand and authentically represents it. Make use of the language they use. Make sure it's in the right tone and method of communication with your target audience.

Focus on the audience

In order to be successful the brand needs to make its main focus to be on the target audience. Instead of being too broad in marketing, narrow the scope. Define the target market and come up with the ideal client. Find out what motivates them and who they are. Once you have discovered exactly who your audience is you can work on discovering their problems.

By figuring out your audience's problems you can then work that into the hook of your brand's story. Do you know what the pain points and concerns of your audience are? If you're not sure then brainstorm or ask them. Work at the list until you have clearly identified problems. The most successful brands intimately understand the problems of their customers.

Values

Explain how customers will benefit from using the brand's products or services. Prioritize their needs and wants over those of the business. Think of them first. Focus on the customers' pain points and how your brand solves them. People will then feel empowered by associating with the brand. Focus on appealing to the customers emotions so that they can feel that bond.

There is a limited window of time to tell a brand story and connect with a customer. Success within that window depends on how much the customer perceives the value offered to be worth. The focus of crafting a brand story should be to define why a customer should care and pay attention. Capture their imagination and focus on the why. The story has to resonate with them. That's achieved by focusing on their why.

Audience solutions

Now that you know the audience's problems, work on being their guide towards the solution. Every story has a guide to the end. Every brand story should guide the audience to the solution. Think of it like being a mentor or waving a magic wand over their problems. Show empathy through your story and present a solution.

Offer a plan

With a solution presented you will also need to offer a plan. Give them clear instructions or a path to follow. They should not feel confused or lost. The goal is to make them see how easy the plan is to follow. That could be something as simple as presenting a three step plan to solving their problem. Be clear and specific so that you eliminate any worries they may have about you. For example:

- Book an appointment
- Let us make a plan for you
- Execute the plan

Call to action

Every story has an end. Much the same, your brand story needs a call to action for its end. Figure out and identify what it is you want your ideal customer to do. That could be visiting a website, making a call or buying from you. Naturally that needs to be clear to them and also it needs to be worth their time. Incentivise them by showing benefits or offering some added value.

Brand Psychology

Everyday we make so many choices. Those choices are based on our feelings and how we perceive ourselves and others around us. The same can be said for making brand choices. Brands are very similar to people. Strong loyalty to a brand as we have seen is the result of good relationships between the brand and the customer. Resulting positive emotions are associated with the brand. Imagine the same is true with interpersonal relations. We are drawn to people whom we have positive associations to. It's no different when it comes to marketing a brand. Positive emotional associations influence customer loyalty and trust.

Utilization of such positive emotions puts customers in a happy comfort zone around the brand and this builds loyalty. Understanding who the audience is and then understanding their values is crucial here. Our values define our identity and shape how we see the world. A successful brand needs to define the values it shares with their audience and make sure it matches theirs. That's how a tribe of loyal customers is built. After all, people perceive brands as humans. Therefore the brand needs to recognize the human relationships and emotions conveyed with their customers.

Emotions

Emotions are at the center of brand choice. Without realizing it many customers choose a brand not because of how good it is for a particular need but rather how it makes them feel. Evidence suggests that the behaviours and decisions of consumers are heavily influenced by emotions. Rather than facts or information consumers are more likely to evaluate a brand based on emotions. For example Nike sneakers make you feel cool and fit in with the fashion trends. Or Starbucks makes you feel hip and sophisticated.

Successful brands are well aware that customers are driven by their emotions. Consequently they focus on the feelings a product or services offer and ensure that positive emotions are associated with them. That's why celebrities are often connected with brands. People have positive emotions associated with those celebrities. That creates more affinity for a brand. Or it's why brands put logos everywhere. It associates positive emotions in the context of where you see it. For example Red Bull is an energy drink. They often sponsor extreme sports events. Adrenaline is high at those events so when people subconsciously see that Red Bull logo they associate it with high adrenaline and positive emotions.

To truly capture the hearts and minds of customers brands need to go beyond good services and build strong emotional connections. Work on making it stronger and don't let them wander. Strong emotional connections can result in brand ambassadors who go as far as spreading the good word about brands. For those super customers extra incentives and bonuses should be sent. Remember their important events, birthdays and communicate well with them.

Social identity

Have you ever felt a connection with people who use a certain kind of computer or car for example? That is social identity in branding. Social identity is how people define themselves based on being part of specific social groups or hierarchies. One might derive social identity from working for a company, being part of a sports team or college and so on. For branding it is highly relevant because social groups have a huge influence on consumer choices.

Advertising campaigns and marketing strategies often capitalize on this fact. Through suggestions that certain social groups identify with products or services. Brands even go as far as forming social groups for their products. Just think of Apple who have focused on compatibility and convenience between their products - no need to go elsewhere. At the end of the day people want to feel connected to others. It's human nature. This is a concept that all brands should be aware of.

Feel

Consequently our choice of brand is based on how we feel and see ourselves with a brand. Marketing efforts of a brand who pay attention to this and focus on customer identity and emotions instead of features tend to build stronger brands. By meeting the needs of a customer a critical step is taken. However the pace and change of customer needs is moving fast. Brands need to be in anticipation and aware of forthcoming movements. Think about why customers come to a brand. Are the products or services of value to them? In what ways? Define why they would pay for it. A strong brand can then build their offers around meeting such needs.

Status

Humans are biologically wired to seek approval from peers and to impress others. That's why social media is so popular. It plays on our desires to be perceived as having status and power. Brand identity is relevant to this. A well thought out brand conveys a status to its consumers. When they use that brand they should feel it brings them status. Those Gucci sneakers make you fit in with the cool crowd. Staying at The Hilton gives you status. Work on building status into a brand and it will allow you to stand out. Plus you will be able to charge a premium price for it. Utilize choice of words and design to be sophisticated, stylish and relevant to the target audiences. Consumers will become more loyal and start to display your products in public.

Create an experience

For users of a brand it should be a psychological experience. Again functionally is not important, it's the feeling and the experience. Consider the psychology of your target audience. What makes them tick? How can you make them feel something? Forget cold hard logic and technological advantages here. Because ultimately you're dealing with humans. Brands should focus on a human experience regardless of their industry or niche. Consumers want to feel understood. Therefore understand and empathize with them.

Part Five: The Secrets of Building Timeless Brands

Reputation Matters

Whatever industry you are in, reputation matters. At the end the reputation of your brand and it's credibility is based on essential establishment of trust with customers. It is what helps them to choose one brand over another. With the rise of the internet and social media never before has this been more important. When a customer is considering buying a service or product they will usually do a quick search online before making a purchase. Information about brands is readily available and easy to access online. Plus customers can easily leave feedback on a brand. If there is nothing much said about a brand or if it's mostly negative then naturally this will impact buying decisions. It all adds up.

Therefore it is essential to a brand's success to portray the best reputation possible.

Particular attention should be focused on the brands online presence, websites and social media. Search up on your brand and take note of any associated posts, blogs or websites. Do they positively represent your brand? Keep up to date with developments. Set up Google Alerts so that you are notified whenever your brand comes up in a new search result. Consider hiring professional agencies to assist with managing this.

Customer Loyalty

Finally, it's all about having loyal customers. When customers have a positive association with a brand it is defined as brand loyalty. Those customers will become repeat customers who stay loyal to the brand. This is demonstrated in their repeat purchases even when competitors are attempting to lure them away. Brand loyalty is big business and brands invest heavily into their customer services in order to establish and maintain customer loyalty. A great example would be Apple who have become iconic due to customer loyalty even over other potentially cheaper alternatives. Customers still commit regardless of price.

Once a customer becomes loyal to a brand they will keep purchasing usually out of convenience of not having to compare or shop around. Simply because they know it works for them. Brands know this and make use of in house features, add ons and limited compatibility with other devices, products or services. In addition they make use of advertising and marketing campaigns to target specific segments of the market who have the potential to become loyal customers. They will cleverly employ tactics to make them more relatable and to connect with the customers.

With consistency, customers become more comfortable relating to a brand. As such all communications should be consistent. Understand customer needs and be giving. Great brands communicate in the same way as friends would to each other. You know how it feels to be marketed to. That feeling when you know someone is trying to sell you something or worse rip you off. Compare it to how a friend talks to you. Big difference. Assume a relationship or friendship and value them.

Marketing departments are constantly analyzing consumer buying trends. These are presented in behaviours and habits of consumers over time. Some are static and some evolve. Collecting such data allows brands to devise marketing and advertising to meet those activities and habits of customers. This in turn helps them to tap into new markets. Once a brand is established it is less work to maintain. Acquiring a customer requires more effort than keeping one. As long as the brand quality remains the same or better, customers won't want to seek alternatives. So how to get those loyal customers?

Provide excellent customer service

One of the most effective tactics of establishing brand loyalty is by providing excellent customer service. This can be what sets a brand apart from the rest. We all know how frustrating customer service can be. Bad reputations can quickly spread. Excellent customer service should include a feedback system for customers. Dedicated staff should be responsible for taking action on that feedback. All this should be conducted in a timely and professional manner.

Failure to ignore trends, research and feedback results in the loss of reputation. In effect brand loyalty is also compromised. Eventually it all affects the bottom line and profits will evaporate.

Brands need to keep up with the evolving market and pay attention to their customers. Ultimately they need to stay relevant and keep providing value. Free marketing is the result of a positive online reputation and it spreads. The more positivity you garner the further it goes. Invest in having the best quality services and products. Then your business is likely to grow more and more.

Programs

Incentivise customers to stay loyal. They can be updated with new promotions, rewards and loyalty programs. For example many brands utilize point based rewards programs. When customers use their services they earn points. Clearly this keeps them coming back for more.

Providing customers with incentives makes them appreciate the brand. It goes above and beyond what they would expect. Customers like to feel like they are exclusive. Give them the VIP feel. Newsletters and memberships are great for this. Let them be the first to know about new deals, rewards, promotions and so on.

Community

Furthermore, successful brands create a community for their customers. They are aware of the holidays and birthdays of their customers. They are always presenting great bonuses to them. Look to surprise them. Make them feel special. Feature their stories and share their pictures of them engaging with your brand. Communication with customers helps to strengthen the relationship. Brands can achieve this through their marketing. Ask for feedback, reply to customers and also engage in forums where they frequent.

Social media is an excellent platform for building a brand community. Make use of platforms such as Facebook groups. Everyone likes to feel wanted. It will make brands feel more personalized, relatable and build loyalty. Speak to them as humans. All of this will create an ecosystem of positive marketing. Eventually customers will spread the good word with their friends and family.

Quality

Never let customers down because of quality. Brand loyalty requires delivering on promises. That means quality must be upholded. Services and products need to be set against and consistently meet high standards. Quality is everything. Strong brands add value and exceed client expectations of quality. Additionally they are consistent in those efforts. Once customer expectations are met or exceeded they should never be lowered. Achieving this requires consistency in everything a brand does. Successful brands uphold their reputations through such consistency and quality control. Never let the standards down. Ever.

Reviews

Reviews are a powerful tool that can build or destroy reputations. Customers often use them to find out whether or not a business is any good. Customers will also give feedback on products or services through reviews. Make sure you do great things and deal with any problems as they arise. If you have no reviews then work on getting some. There are many groups of leading reviewers in every industry that you can reach out to and instigate reviews from. Make use of email lists and so on to drive more reviews.

Google is one of the main review platforms. They allow you to list businesses and then on Google Maps people can see reviews for that particular listing. If you have a set business location then make use of this. If you don't have a set location then Facebook is more suitable. Have a page where people can leave reviews and interact with your brand. Additionally if you sell on platforms such as Amazon then work on getting great reviews there. Encourage people to leave reviews and try to get their emails.

Taking things further you can build even more social proof by asking your customers to for example post pictures of themselves with you tagged in the post. Ask them to post pictures of them using your products or services. That will be more great social proof.

These strategies will help you to develop and maintain a good reputation online. Overall it's not too much work. Otherwise consider hiring a professional digital marketing agency. Ultimately you need to stop being reactive to building a reputation and instead take an active approach. Take responsibility for it.

"It takes 20 years to build a reputation and five minutes to ruin it." Warren Buffet

Dealing with negative reviews

Reputations can be easily damaged by negative reviews. When dealing with them you need to remain calm and level headed the whole time. Don't rule out that customer entirely. Take action and respond in a polite and professional manner. Depending on the context you can respond to them in private or public. If you think it is unfair then flag the review to the administrators. Learn and grow from the experience.

Valued

Focusing on providing great customer experiences as opposed to driving sales is a great way of ensuring brand loyalty. Too many brands focus on getting as much revenue as possible. Customers dislike being taken advantage of and it won't take long before they have drained that customer and the bad word has spread. It will be the downfall of many brands. Instead by focusing on service it reminds customers that they are valued. As such it makes them feel more committed to that brand. Think about how much value you can add instead of how much profit you can take. Add as much value to them as possible through the products and services of the brand. The money will come, don't worry.

In the end brand loyalty is vital. It is what sets a brand apart from the rest and keeps those customers coming back. They don't need to be convinced by expensive advertising or clever marketing tactics. Once a customer is acquired they are easier to keep. As long as the brand delivers. Consumer surveys by Yotpo have proven that "nearly eighty percent of customers consider themselves loyal to a brand after around three purchases." Good deals and quality are usually what locks them in and keeps them coming back for more. Ensure that everyone working for the brand helps to maintain the high standard and to keep providing outstanding customer services.

Progress Audits

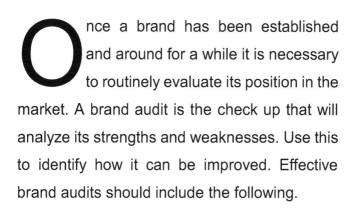

Once a brand has been established and around for a while it is necessary to routinely evaluate its position in the market. A brand audit is the check up that will analyze its strengths and weaknesses. Use this to identify how it can be improved. Effective brand audits should include the following.

- Internal branding: Included values, mission and culture of brand
- External branding: Included externals such as online presence, logo, design, advertising, marketing, public relations and so on.
- Customer experience: Includes sales conversion process, customer services and support.

All of the above can be analyzed internally or by a specialist marketing company. There are a number of metrics that should be considered when measuring. To begin with, a framework should be established. Consider who the target customers are, the market itself and the marketing plan to reach them. An effective brand audit will identify where a brand is being successful and any other areas for improvement. Consider the following.

Customer feedback

The customer always comes first. Question them. Numbers alone aren't enough for a successful audit. You will need customer feedback. This will give a more rounded and personal feedback. Customers will offer information that cannot always be shown through data. Contact your customers by surveying them. Leave a feedback form on your website and social media channels. Send out surveys via email and ask your loyal customers to give their feedback. Make use of services catered for this such as SmartSurvey to create specific online questionnaires. Are customers happy with what you're offering? They should be satisfied with the value and that will keep them coming back.

External marketing materials

Analyze any external marketing materials. These are things such as the advertising you put out in the real world. Business cards, brochures, packaging and so on. Are they working for you? Could they be improved? Are they relevant to the current market? Some may indeed need to be revamped and modernized according to the current market.

Online analytics

Since we know that the majority of customers research online before making purchases then we know how important online data can be. Take a look at the analytics of your website to determine how well it is performing. Analyze if your SEO is working or if the advertising campaigns are working. Monitor where traffic is coming from. Identify exactly where your web traffic is coming from. Should it be found that web traffic is limited to a few sources then it would be a good idea to think of ways to diversify. Traffic should come from multiple sources. Analyze if any traffic sources have dropped off or increased. Take a look at click through rates. Google offers some useful tools for such analysis.

Determine bounce rate or how quickly visitors leave your site. The longer they stay the better and that would depend on how engaging the content is. How about conversion rates? Are they improving or not? Find out how many people visit the site each month. Find out how long they stay. Find out if they access the site on mobile, tablet or computer. Gain as much information as you can. After all, if you have invested heavily into a website you want to be sure it is working for your brand. Nowadays the brand website is a central pillar of brand identity.

Social media analytics

Additional audience data can be discovered through social media analytics. Social media allows brands to discover key metrics about their audiences. For example, find out where they are based, what their interests and backgrounds are. Discover what makes them engage more. Identify what doesn't work and go all in on what does. Find out as much as is provided through the metrics available. This will help paint a clear picture of the direction to head in.

Maintaining social media presence requires consistent efforts. It's easy to become irrelevant and fall into obscurity. Be sure to thoroughly check up on your brand's social media. Whatever your platform is, find out which posts are creating the most engagement. Metrics to consider would be views, comments, shares and likes. Also if you use multiple social media platforms make sure that your brand is somewhat consistent in its marketing across those platforms. Use the same logo, profile pictures, taglines and so on.

Sales data

Sales data is something that should be monitored at least monthly. Clearly this will give you feedback on if the business is profitable or not. Naturally there will be trends and cycles in the markets. Some markets can be seasonable and this should be factored in. If sales are dropping or increasing then discover why.

Measuring Brand Awareness

Brand awareness can seem like a vague idea that can be difficult to be measured with metrics. But still you need to know whether or not your efforts are working. So how do you know if you need to change something? Although it is difficult to measure you can still get a gauge on it through some key ways. For example, have you seen more traffic since your efforts? A rise in traffic is a good sign that you're doing the right thing. If your traffic is the same or worse then consider revising your strategy.

If you used advertising in your brand awareness campaigns then you can analyze advertising metrics to determine if they were successful or not. Did you get good click through rates and retention? If you focus on social media campaigns then there are many metrics which you can analyze. Did you get shared a lot? Did you get many likes and comments? Use the results to adjust your efforts going forwards.

Take action

Once completed a brand audit should have identified any areas on where to take action. That could be anything from adjusting prices to marketing strategies and ao on. Detailed research will provide key areas and targets to focus on. Put together a plan of action and start moving forward on improving the brand. Keep tweaking the metrics and stats that serve and are most relevant to the brand. Continually update the brand to match up to new information. Remember an audit should not just be a one time thing. Try to do them at least once a year. It will help to keep your brand fresh.

The process of building brand awareness may seem overwhelming but it is what will help consumers remember your brand. Spend quality time on building your brand. It is what will move the needle. This isn't a one time job. In fact brand awareness is an ongoing process. Markets change and we have to adapt. Keep learning and growing.

Common Branding Mistakes

E very business makes branding mistakes. Even those Top Fortune 100 companies. When building brands there are some common pitfalls and failings to be aware of. To help you avoid making branding mistakes here are some of the most common branding mistakes.

No awareness

An unknown brand is destined for failure. If no one knows you even exist then no one is ever going to buy from you. If you're facing this problem then the solution is to raise awareness. Make sure you have a solid online presence.

Make sure you are posting content. Make sure you're asking people to share about you. Spread the word.

Having a clear and consistent identity will define how well the brand impacts the public. Identify what the brand stands for and how it sets out to achieve its goals. Make sure the reasons are big and clear.

No engagement

In some cases you may get a decent amount of attention but it fades away. That's because it is not engaging enough. It's like a pretty face without personality. The pretty face will hook you in but will the personality keep you? If you're struggling to keep customers engaged then consider making your brand more interactive. Create contests, surveys, quizzes and actions that require engagement.

Create a buzz around your brand by engaging with consumers. Focus on interactive and engaging customers. Respond to their comments. Create groups where customers can interact with your brand. Spread news and add value to the community.

Too many brands focus on connecting with customers only when it comes time to make a sale. Go the extra mile and be more social. Keep posting on your social media channels. Engage with your audience. Talk about the things they care about and ask for their feedback. Try to make friends with them instead of just trying to take their money.

Not enough content

Many brands make the mistake of not publishing enough content. Maybe they start off strong but it tails off quite quickly. Our current media environment is changing everyday and you need to keep up to stay relevant. Persist when you're not getting results at the start. With consistency traction will pick up.

Be shareable

Whatever your industry or niche is, your content should be easy to share. Sharing makes things go viral. Whatever your posting, make sure it is shareable. Word of mouth will spread news about your brand like a wildfire. People will want to find out all about why this hot brand. All you need to do is make awesome content then leave buttons to share and ask people to share.

The wrong audience

A common problem is that your brand is attracting the wrong people. Keep an eye on your analytics and make sure that the target audience is being reached. If they are not then you need to consider revising the methods you use to target them. Test out different regions and messages. Get creative and adapt.

The wrong platforms

Now some brands are going to be more suited to particular channels. For example clothing works well on Instagram whilst technology would be a better fit on YouTube. At the beginning you can experiment with a bunch of platforms. After a while it will be clear which one is more relevant. Go all in on that and stick with it. Work on constantly improving.

Being too generic

A strong brand identity is the one that stands out from the competition. They do something different. They look and feel different. Those generic brands are the ones that get lost in the crowd and fail to stand out. Do your research on the market. Look at the ways you can stand out. That could be something as simple as color. Or maybe it's the brand voice. Whatever it is, don't be generic. Find a way to stand out.

Inconsistency

Successful brands are consistent. Just look at Coca-Cola, it's everywhere and it's been everywhere consistently for years. That has helped it to become the giant it now is. Behind those long lasting brands is a clear and consistent identity. Maintain that whatever the medium or platform you're working on.

Establish how you want your brand to be perceived and stick with it. Make sure that perception is consistent in everything it does both online and offline. Customers will associate this with a strong and trustworthy brand.

Lack of direction

Knowing your brand identity intrinsically is great but if no one else knows it then it's destined to fail. Great brands require great direction. Those responsible for the direction should make sure the brand identity is represented authentically by its partners and team members. Make sure they are all on board and know it as well as the brand director does. Again this is where brand guidelines and brand guides are an excellent idea.

Furthermore, some brands have become so iconic due to the people and faces behind them. Just think of Steve Jobs or Bill Gates. They got behind their brands. In turn this added more personality to the brands. Don't be afraid to represent your brand and put your face out there.

Evolution

Consumer trends and tastes will change over time. That's a fact. To accommodate that fact successful brands need to be able to adapt. Now that doesn't necessarily mean taking things apart completely. Sometimes you just need to revamp a little and refresh things here and there. That could be a visual refresh or a new offer and so on. Keep an eye on the trends and evolve with them. Be ready for them and look to the future.

Whilst it's important not to jump on the bandwagon it's also important to not ignore trends. Some trends may indeed be beneficial for your brand. Look out for new trends that relate to your brand and take advantage of them. Sure jumping on a trend can help with brand awareness. However this should not sacrifice the integrity of the brand and go against its values. Some trends may damage your brand. Avoid anything political or controversial. Competing in a market requires brands to constantly monitor changes in the market and consumer behaviours. Keep an eye on competitors and how to improve on them.

Keep an eye on consumer needs and wants. Be able to accommodate any changes.

When making changes it's important to do it correctly. Be sure that any changes are worth the risk of potentially losing business. If you are considering changes, get feedback on them first from the team and loyal customers. Should you be rebranding make sure that everything gets rebranded. Inform your audience and make them part of the journey. As markets change and brands develop it's always important to hold true to the original values. A well planned mission statement should serve as a reminder to stay true and on track.

Always value staff and customers

The people who work for a brand are also the voice of it. They embody and live it. They should champion it. In order to do that they need to feel valued so that they feel happy and enjoy working for the brand.

Moving on, customers are the end recipients of the brand. They are the reason the brand exists. They need to also feel valued and happy to purchase from the brand. Think from their perspective and value them.

Failure to monitor progress

Keeping track of how a brand progresses is essential to its growth. Monitoring progress helps brands to stay relevant and keep delivering to their customers. Make sure to complete regular audits and monitor progress.

Reputation

Inevitably at some point you're going to get bad reviews. As a brand you need to deal with reviews as constructive feedback. Don't argue with customers. Try to listen to them and see how you can improve. Reply calmly, respectfully and in a timely manner. If you feel they are wrong then raise an issue with the place where a review was left.

Additionally, many brands are so focused on their online reputation that they forget about the offline reputation. Make sure that your business has a good reputation in person. People should be staying positive about it. A strong brand culture compels people to buy from the brand whilst building trust and reputation both in the market and within the brands team.

Always make sure that your branding strategy matches how you want to be perceived. Keep investing in your brand awareness and watch it grow. As a brand that works on being the best it can be, it's important to never break promises. When you start out don't set unrealistic ambitions that are impossible to deliver on. Be authentic and make sure those promises are ones that can be fulfilled. Everyone working for the brand should uphold its reputation and promises.

Conclusion

L adies and gentlemen, we've arrived at the conclusion of this book. There has been so much discussed up to this point. Which makes it a great time to now summarize and conclude the most important messages and promises that were made at the start of this book.

The main goal of this book was to detail how to make your brand successful and stand out. We're living in a crazy world with so much information, competition and thriving marketplaces. Consumers are overwhelmed. No longer are they as receptive to advertising from just some random brand. It's not the way it used to be with a few advertising campaigns and much less competitors. As businesses we need to build brands that customers have positive associations with and trust. This will influence them to buy from us. That brand will be trusted with loyal customers who will want to choose you over the others. In this book that's what was presented. Now let's summarize the key points.

To begin with I introduced you to what the brand is and why it matters. In that chapter it was explained that the brand is more than just a logo or a name. In summary the brand is what sells the product or services. It's about making a promise on what people believe it is. We have certain associations with brands and building a successful brand requires making those associations positive. Building such a reputation is going to require persistence, hard work and passion. Consumers need to believe in the brand. Strong brands know this and it makes selling much easier. Without that known brand you will struggle to sell.

What this requires are some steps. First it's about creating a brand character. This is a set of human characteristics and attributes to help position brands in the market. Such character helps brands to stand out from the competitors. Essentially it's about defining why your brand is better or rather defining a unique selling proposition (USP). Define, why is it better than other brands? Such an understanding requires you to know what your customers want, the capabilities of your brand and the position of your brand against competitors.

With these things in mind we moved onto explaining how to create your brand identity and what makes it up. We talked about the brand elements and the things that form it's whole identity. Once you've got that together we explored how to create a brand guide so that everyone in the team understands how the brand should be represented publicly. All of these things should be consistent across the different platforms, messaging, marketing and advertising of the brand.

Moving onto part two we talked about why market research is essential to brand success. I showed you how to conduct strengths, weaknesses, opportunities and threats analysis. Next it's really important to understand your audience. You need to really discover who your ideal customer would be. I showed you how to obtain the most vital information in a number of ways so that you can fully understand your target audience. In turn the best value can be delivered to them. Furthermore you're going to need to analyse the competition and I showed you how to do that in addition to how you can find out who they are. Learning everything you need to know about competitors will help with positioning your brand as being a better choice. There was then a chapter about extended market research using the top websites. Information on market research across Google, Facebook, YouTube, Instagram and Amazon is included here.

Moving onto part three I showed you how to develop a strategy and stand out. A brand strategy will help your brand to stand out from all the others. There are a number of important things to consider when putting a strategy together. Those were discussed here. I also showed you some really useful information about pricing strategies. This is another key way for brands to compete. People often make choices based on pricing. Successful brands are able to determine the value of their services and products for their target audience. To help you determine yours there are pricing analysis, strategies tools and techniques outlined in that chapter.

Moving on I talked about what makes brands stand out in a crowded marketplace. Now more than ever it's becoming increasingly difficult to stand out. But with the right knowledge there are still ways that you can make your brand stand out. Those along with the steps were discussed in that chapter. Staying relevant and adapting with the change in markets was also discussed. In addition, what makes content go viral was presented here. For a brand producing content you need to be aware of getting the best reach. There are a number of ways that you can do that. From using emotions to being useful, utilising triggers and much more.

In part four I discussed how to create your brand journey. Stories are a powerful way of building emotional connections and as humans we are deeply affected by them. Stories are great for putting your brand out there in the perception of the public eye. It will help you to establish long term trust with your customers and loyalty. Brands need to go beyond advertising and marketing campaigns. They need to be relatable and demonstrate value through their stories. Focus on the audience, find out what their pain points are, present solutions, offer plans and have a call to action. Also you need to have psychology behind that to understand the emotions of your customers. Make them happy and in turn create loyalty.

In the last part of the book we talked about longevity. We talked about why reputation is important and why you should pay attention to the whole of your brand's perception. Continually developing customer loyalty should always be a focus to make sure the customer is happy. Listen to them, pay attention to their reviews and deal with them professionally. In addition, conduct regular progress audits as a part of your brand's evolution. This will ensure that you're consistently delivering value. Finally I showed you some of the most common branding mistakes to avoid and to be aware of. At the end every brand makes mistakes. So you need to be aware of the common pitfalls that you may come across

In summary you discovered in this book how to build a successful and long-lasting brand. Whether you are a new brand or one that wants to reinvent. Take the information that you've learned here which is going to give you specific ways to stand out, be more unique and offer the most value to your consumers. What I promised you was if you clearly understand your audience and how your brand is unique it will make yours a much better choice. Customers are going to be loyal to you. With loyal customers your brand will keep growing because they'll become your patrons. They will promote and share your good reputation. That's going to keep growing organically and the good word will spread. Leading you to in turn have more influence, purchases, longevity and happy customers.

Now once again there are no shortcuts to this and it won't happen overnight. But if you follow the knowledge in this book then inevitably you will build a successful brand. Make no mistake, it will require trial-and-error plus time. But stick with it. Focus on having a strong identity. Focus on delivering the most value and being the best brand you can be. Craft your brand based on those principles. I wish you longevity and success!

Bonus: Brand Research Examples

What follows is a system of analyzing brands. This is going to give you an idea of how to build a brand. I have included both personal and business brands here. First we will choose a brand and conduct a Google search to identify the main channels plus information about the brand. Those would be the ones that they are directly controlling such as their website or social media channels.

Moving on we will analyze the color schemes, design and logo themes. Take note of the three main things you notice across the board on all of their channels. Record the type of language, slogans, tag lines and descriptions they are using. Are they formal? Are they specific to their industry?

Next take a look at the kinds of products and/or services they sell. Do they have any publications? Perhaps they are a service based business. Or they could be a combination of products and services. Who is their target market? Identify the market of the brand. Are they male or female? What age range? Add as much relevant information here as possible to paint a picture of their ideal customer.

Moving on, identify the customer journey. How does the customer find them? This could be from organic searches, referrals, social media and so on. Finally take note of how the customer makes purchasing decisions, and ultimately buys your product and/or service.

Now let's look at some examples to help you understand how to analyze brands.

Brand: Mike Thurston

About

- https://www.instagram.com/mikethurston

- https://www.youtube.com/channel/UCz GLDaTu81nJDtWK10MniGg

- https://www.mikethurston.co.uk/

- https://web.facebook.com/mikethurston official

Identity

What are the main things you notice across the board?

- Use of his body
- High quality images and videos
- Professional edits

Voice

- Informal
- Natural
- Unique

- Gym terms

Products and/or services
- Training plans
- Branded clothes
- Affiliate products

Publications
- None

Target market
- Male
- Gym members.

The Customer Journey

How does the customer find them?
- Youtube - trending, collabs
- Instagram - trending, collabs
- Google - keywords

How does the customer make purchasing decisions?

- Instagram - Website links in bio. He develops trust and relationships
- YouTube - Develops audience relationships. Engaging content. Links to stuff he sells.

What can you learn from this? What are the key points?

Have an engaged following. A percentage of followers are going to buy from you. The more the better. Produce high quality content that resonates with them and offers value. Build trust.

Brand: Tiesto

About

- https://twitter.com/tiesto
- https://www.facebook.com/tiesto/
- https://www.tiesto.com/
- https://open.spotify.com/artist/2o5jDhtH VPhrJdv3cEQ99Z
- https://www.instagram.com/tiesto/

Identity

- Consistent branding across all platforms.
- Promotes his latest song. Uses it in headers, profile and bio.
- Personalized posts. Mixture of lifestyle. Dj, business

Voice

- A focus on engagement and audience feedback
- Questions and polls

Products and/or services

- Dj shows - Pushing through songs and engagement

Publications

- Music releases

Target market

- Party people
- Music fans

The Customer Journey

How does the customer find them?

- Twitter, Facebook, Instagram and socials fed by Soundcloud, Spotify, YouTube and music
- People who hear his music then seek him out, follow him and support his music which increases his reach, popularity and show fee.

How does the customer make purchasing decisions?

- They become fans of him that want to see him live. If he shows up in their town then they would be likely to buy a ticket.

What can you learn from this? What are the key points?

- Post engaging content
- Keep your branding goals consistent across platforms
- Use a mix of informal, formal and fun content
- Build a loyal fanbase

Brand: Bumble

About

- Bumble app
- Bumble IG
- Bumble FB
- Bumble website

Identity

- Consistent branding and color. Clear and obvious

Voice

- Logical

Products and/or services they sell

- Paid plans

Publications

- n/a

Target market

- Singles

The Customer Journey

How does the customer find them?

After leaving Tinder Wolf Herd founded Bumble which is also a similar dating application where users can swipe left or right. But the conversation can only be started by women. Ladies first. Wolfe Herd applied the same strategy of marketing the app to college campuses. It gained traction and soon reached over 100,000 downloads.

Since Bumble is very similar to Tinder it would need some help to become popular. To achieve this they focused on offering better quality matches between users. Bumble offers much more information than Tinder. For example, job, interest and so on. All of which make the match up process more effective. The great thing about this is that people would talk about having much better success on Bumble versus other apps. So then one of the most powerful forms of marketing comes into play, word of mouth.

How does the customer make purchasing decisions?

Bumble is free of charge to download along with all of its main features. Monetization comes through purchasing special features to enhance user experience on the app. Those include subscription models and various in-app purchases.

What can you learn from this? What are the key points?

- Building apps requires starting with small groups and spreading it through word of mouth.
- Think of the customer and add value

Brand: GymShark

About
- https://uk.gymshark.com/
- https://www.instagram.com/gymshark/

Identity
- Clean, simple and appealing to fitness lovers.

Voice
- Simple and use of fitness terminology.

Products and/or services
- Clothing, applications, accessories,

Publications
- None

Target market
- Fitness enthusiasts

The Customer Journey

How does the customer find them?

Gymshark was successful in large part due to building a community of influencers. Early on they partnered with well known social media influencers. They sponsored them and this led to wider exposure. Followers of those influencers are fans of them and will happily use the products they do. In addition GymShark saw a gap in the market that was missing. Decent quality gym clothing that looks great.

How does the customer make purchasing decisions?

Social proof by influencers.

Ease of buying.

What can you learn from this? What are the key points?

- Influencers make a significant impact. But don't try to just use an influencer for attention. Instead focus on building long lasting mutually beneficial relationships. Invest in the process and think long term.

- Make it easy for the customer.
- Documenting the brand's journey allows its customers to feel like they are on the inside. Such transparency is great because it builds trust.

References

Ogilvy, D. (2011). *Ogilvy on advertising*. Prion.

Kotler, P. (2005). According to Kotler: The world's foremost authority on Marketing answers your questions. AMACOM.

Larson, K., Hazlett, R. L., Chaparro, B. S., & Picard, R. W. (n.d.). Measuring the aesthetics of reading. People and Computers XX — Engage, 41–56. https://doi.org/10.1007/978-1-84628-664-3_4

Trademarks. United States Patent and Trademark Office - An Agency of the Department of Commerce. (2021, July 2). https://www.uspto.gov/trademarks.

Mohsin, M. (2021, June 30). 10 Instagram statistics you need to know in 2021 [NEW

DATA]. Oberlo.
https://www.oberlo.com/blog/instagram-stats-every-marketer-should-know.

Select your location and language. FedEx Global Home - Select Your Location. (n.d.). http://www.fedex.com/.

Order pizza & pasta online for Carryout & delivery - Domino's Pizza. Domino's Pizza, Order Online. (n.d.). https://www.dominos.com/.

Free shipping – no minimum. The North Face®. (n.d.). https://www.thenorthface.com/.

Connors, R. J. (2014). Warren Buffett on Business: Principles from the Sage of Omaha. John Wiley & Sons.

Polkes, A. (2020, December 9). The state of brand loyalty 2021: Global consumer survey.

Yotpo. https://www.yotpo.com/blog/the-state-of-brand-loyalty-2021-global-consumer-survey/.

Start Your Week The Right Way

Hey everyone!

Thanks for buying this book. You can keep upto date with me on my YouTube channel. Every week I post new videos about business, lifestyle and success.

Thomas Swain YouTube

It's a way to start your week off with a bang. And fill yourself with ideas that could potentially change everything.

Thomas Swain YouTube